Sailing

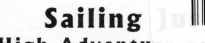

High Adventure on a Small Budget

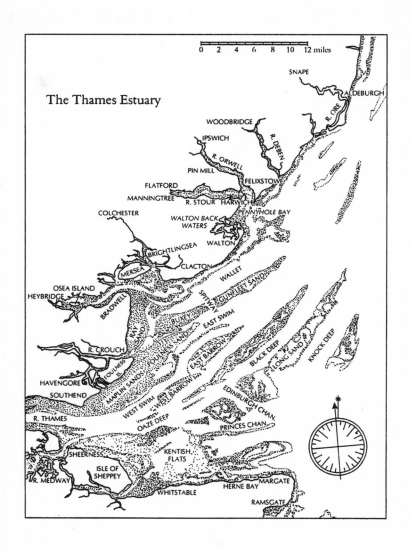

The Thames Estuary

0 2 4 6 8 10 12 miles

SNAPE
ALDEBURGH
R. ORE
WOODBRIDGE
IPSWICH
R. DEBEN
R. ORWELL
PIN MILL
FELIXSTOWE
FLATFORD
MANNINGTREE
R. STOUR HARWICH
COLCHESTER
PENNYHOLE BAY
WALTON BACK
WATERS
BRIGHTLINGSEA
WALTON
MERSEA
CLACTON
WALLET
OSEA ISLAND
HEYBRIDGE
BRADWELL
SWIN
GUNFLEET SAND
BUXEY
EAST SWIM
RAY SAND
FOULNESS SAND
EAST BARROW
BLACK DEEP
LONG SAND
KNOCK DEEP
R. CROUCH
FOULNESS IS.
HAVENGORE
MAPLIN SANDS
WEST BARROW
SOUTHEND
WEST SWIM
EDINBURGH CHAN.
R. THAMES
OAZE DEEP
PRINCES CHAN.
SHEERNESS
KENTISH FLATS
ISLE OF SHEPPEY
R. MEDWAY
MARGATE
HERNE BAY
WHITSTABLE
RAMSGATE

Sailing Just For Fun
High Adventure on a Small Budget

A.C. Stock

ILLUSTRATED

SEAFARER BOOKS
2002

First Published 1998
Minerva Press

This edition published in 2002 in the UK by
Seafarer Books
102 Redwald Road,
Rendlesham,
Woodbridge,
Suffolk, IP12 2TE

2nd impression 2005

UK ISBN 0 9538180 6 3

Cover design by Louis Mackay
Photos and illustrations by A. C. Stock

Printed in Finland by WS Bookwell, OY

This is a book for the man who has read all the 'How to' books and still finds that he cannot. It is unashamedly simple, basic and old fashioned. In it I dwell on my own area, the Thames Estuary, and my own little gaff cutter, *Shoal Waters*, for these are the things that I know about. The reader will find no reference to ship to shore radio, kicking straps, self steering gear or even engines for I use none of them in my maritime wanderings. I don't say that you should not have them, just that they are not absolutely essential and are very expensive. You will find no mention of 'safety equipment' as a separate section, for I regard everything on the boat from truck to keel as part and parcel of my safety equipment. It is an interesting point that pre-war sailing books never mention life jackets or flares and I have none. They do emphasise non-slip decks, on which I insist. Ever seen a safety leaflet advocating fine sand sprinkled on wet paint to give decks a non slip surface? Don't run away with the idea that I am a stick in the mud automatically opposed to every new idea: this is being written on a word processor. I regard Terylene sails and ropes as God's greatest gift to sailors, second only to leak-proof, hot moulded hulls. Nevertheless a lot of good sailing was done without them before they were invented and nothing basic 'twixt wind and sea has changed since they appeared on the chandlers shelves. The lack of them has not prevented my sixteen foot boat covering over sixty-eight thousand miles since she was launched the week before Whitsun 1963. All trips began and finished at Heybridge on the River Blackwater. She has never failed to return there through lack of wind each Sunday evening. In 1970 and again in 1980 I had to leave her away from home due to gales. I believe that it is a record of achievement under sail without equal. It is not that I am particularly clever; it's just that nobody else seems to attempt it. Now that my seventieth birthday is behind me I can face the fact that I am a man of distinctly modest ability in a wide field of human achievement. One successful niche in my life seems to be in getting a small boat from 'A' to 'B' under sail. I suspect that my only advantage over my fellow sailors is the conviction that these trips can be done. In the pages ahead I hope to convince the reader of that fact and introduce him to some of the wrinkles that have helped me on my way. Few are new, but far too many have been forgotten in the white heat of this technological age.

Charles Stock
Shoal Waters
1 January 1997

Contents

Chapter One

The Case for the Small Cruiser

When I launched my new sixteen foot sailing cruiser *Shoal Waters* at the Blackwater Sailing Club near Maldon in 1963 she was obviously small, but not outstandingly so, beside the many yachts already on station. Each winter there was keen competition to get a space in the club workshop to steal a march on the weather. Today most of the craft at the club are too big to get into the old workshop and a new, larger one has had to be built. The boats I meet around the coast seem to be bigger each season. There is no doubt that larger boats give better accommodation, in particular, sufficient room to invite guests to join you for a cruise; but do they give more and better sailing? I think not.

I have never doubted that I could get just as much fun out of a sixty ton ketch in the West Indies as I get out of my sixteen foot cruiser in the Thames Estuary, but it seems to me that there must be some correlation between the size of the boat and the time available to sail her. Of course, the chap with the larger boat has the advantage when it comes to a three or four week summer holiday, but what can he achieve in a weekend that cannot be done in a far smaller boat?

Many of us with dreary undemanding jobs want some sort of a challenge when we go afloat. I find a sixty or seventy mile weekend trip a deeply satisfying achievement. The same trip in a forty foot boat is just a milk run. Remember that the sheer joy of using the wind to travel in delightful maritime surroundings is the main object of the exercise. We must have a life-support system, but it can be a capsule rather than a caravan.

Let me admit that this may be just sour grapes on my part in that I couldn't afford a very much larger boat anyway, but I note that two very experienced sailors at my club, who could well afford larger craft, stick to boats just twenty feet long. The initial capital cost rises sharply with each extra foot of length overall and while few people sell boats at a loss in terms of paper money, those who translate those sums into real purchasing power find less to be smug about. It's just no good comparing today's pound note with the one you had in your pocket five years ago. Compare the number of loaves of sliced bread that you could have bought with the purchase price at that time, with the number the selling price would buy today. All other costs rise in proportion (except perhaps marina charges which often have a minimum charge at twenty or even thirty feet). Insurance, moorings, harbour dues, paint, varnish, antifoulant, replacement sails and rigging, not to mention engine maintenance, tot up to a depressing bill when averaged out over the few days actually spent under way each season.

While a bigger boat may well appear safer (until you fall overboard and try to get back an board over those high topsides), many items of rigging and gear will be renewed less often than those on a small boat, purely and simply because of the cost. A look at the distances sailed by the boats of the East Anglian Offshore Racing Association, fast boats with strong crews, shows a distinct preference for the fifty mile races over the eighty mile ones. Of course these distances are mostly sailed in open waters bordering the North Sea and most of them still race in heavy weather. Few large cruisers take advantage of their capacity to do the same. During the 1975 season *Shoal Waters* sailed some forty weekends and averaged eighty miles a weekend. Of course I spent a lot longer under way but then I like sailing! The difference is that the large boat, once it arrives, anchors or picks up a mooring and stays put until it is time to set off home. The small boat, after recovering from the initial trip to another creek or river, can get under way again near high water to explore one of the interesting creeks in the upper drying reaches. Large boats could do the same, for trading craft drawing at least six feet when fully laden visited mills, wharves and farmers' landing places which are still to be found in such delightful areas but somehow large yachts rarely do so.[1] What prevents them enjoying a quiet sail as the sun goes down behind a lonely sea wall, or drifting with the tide in the calm of early morning to work up an appetite for eggs and bacon, is the sheer hard work of getting a large boat under way just for a short trip. Time and time again I see large boats under motor in perfect sailing conditions, purely and simply because the owners cannot face the work of hoisting and handling large sails (not to mention the heavy anchor).

Big sails cost a lot more than small ones, so a big boat is unlikely to have as full a set as her smaller sister. Perhaps the best example here is the recent fashion for just one roller headsail that can be reefed to any size to suit the wind

---

[1] Some years ago the author sailed to Battlesbridge Mill, ten miles up river from Burnham on Crouch, in company with the America's Cup contender *Victory 82* which drew nine feet!

strength rather than carrying a range of separate sails. God help any poor sailor on such a boat when the gear fails (and all gear will fail sometime) so that his spitfire jib becomes a genoa when it unrolls suddenly in gale force eight.

Big boats need bigger engines. Remember that a sailing boat needs a bigger engine than a motor boat of the same displacement to push her into a head wind because of the windage of the mast and rigging. In the early seventies I left Dover in company with a Twister class yacht when the north-easterly gales, from which we had been sheltering for several days, eased. I was under storm trysail and spitfire jib. They were an elderly couple with a nephew as crew and had decided to travel under motor. The first tack took me out to the South Goodwin light vessel and I overtook them to windward! Mountainous seas had built up in the narrow Dover Straits and their engine would just not keep the vessel head to wind. When I last saw them as darkness closed in, they seemed to be making sail.

Even if the money is available, the disadvantages of larger boats do not end there. More time will have to be spent on maintenance, which means less time for sailing. Much of the savings brought in by the use of fibreglass for hulls instead of traditional wood has already been lost by the avalanche of gadgets from self-steering to microwave ovens, which all need some attention sooner or later. The work of handling these boats, especially sheeting in the big headsails, becomes sheer slavery. Bigger boats generally anchor in deeper water. The anchor and cable will have to be that much larger and that means so many more pounds of galvanised iron to lower into the water and lift out again. The small boat owner will cheerfully use a larger anchor than really needed just to ensure sound sleep on rough nights. Many large boats cut anchor weight as low as they dare and then compound the risk by using warp instead of chain. Of course increasing numbers of modern sailors never anchor, preferring to sail from one marina to the next but even here the small boat often wins. Lock gates are very expensive to install so the entrance to many marinas is over a drying sill which uncovers in time to retain six or eight feet of water at the pontoons. When the sill is underwater a gauge at the side will show the depth available for craft wishing to enter or leave. The smaller, normally shallower boat will be in first and able to leave over a longer period next day. In a crowded area or at bank holidays, the big boat will find it difficult to get a berth, but the little one can always squeeze in somewhere. At Cowes Week, 1977, everywhere was packed with the Admiral's Cup fleet and those who had come south for the Jubilee Fleet Review a few weeks earlier over and above the normal participants. *Shoal Waters* found a drying berth alongside a pontoon at the National Sailing Centre without any trouble.

All in all, the small boat will spend more time under way, she will visit quiet areas beyond the reach of larger craft, and give a much greater impression of speed, insofar as her crew will be sitting that much closer to the water.

Of course there are snags. In a hard beat to windward with a fair tide the large boat wins every way once the waves get up and begin to break. Now the small boat owner plumbs the depths of despair as he battles away on one long, long tack while the big fellow with his private lead mine six feet down in the water makes three boards and fades away over the horizon, so depressingly far ahead. When bad weather comes along, life can get pretty grotty cooped up in a very small boat whether in harbour or under way. It's the old story, you pays your money and takes your choice. All I am trying to prove is that there is plenty of good sailing and pleasure afloat for the chap who can only afford a modest craft.

Chapter Two

My Cruising Area:
Its Effect on Hull and Rig

I suppose that the Thames Estuary starts somewhere between Shoeburyness on the Essex shore and Sheerness in Kent, for hereabouts the sailor who has travelled down from the historic port of London realises that the shore is falling away on either hand. Suddenly he is facing a very wide area of open water! The high ground of the Isle of Sheppey remains a comforting sight away to the south, but the low sea wall protecting the Essex marshes soon fades away in the north. There are another twenty-five miles of Kent running due east to the North Foreland and one of the only two lighthouses in the area. It is forty-five miles north-east to the other one on a low shingle spit called Orfordness. An imaginary line between those two points, bulging in the middle to take in the drying sand called the Kentish Knock, completes a triangle containing some five hundred square miles of prime sailing water. Add twelve widely differing rivers with a total navigable length of some one hundred and eighty miles, a further twenty-five miles of canals, splatter some thirty or forty sand banks offshore, spice the whole lot with the relics and traditions of two thousand years of warfare, trade and fishing; top up with prevailing offshore winds, the best summer weather in Britain together with gentle but useful tides that come and go in a logical fashion and you have something approaching the ideal playground for small boat sailors.

There is another important feature that is largely unrecognised: the shock absorber effect of the drying banks as they emerge from the sea twice each day. Perhaps the worst time to be at sea in a small boat is after a long blow, when the heavy swell persists and shakes the wind out of the sails so that the boat cannot maintain steerage way. Such a swell can last for days in some areas. In the Thames Estuary, all that energy is dissipated in surf on the sands and the swell has often gone twenty-four hours after the wind eases.

In early March 1980 *Radio Caroline*, the pirate radio ship *Mi Amigo*, broke her moorings and drove onto the Longsand in a north-easterly gale late on Wednesday night. She was swept by mountainous seas and sank in thirty feet of water. On Friday evening I went straight to the boat from the office and sailed to the river mouth. At high water at 0500 hrs Saturday morning I sailed from Bradwell for a mill pond trip covering some forty miles outside the river to find and photograph the wreck. By high water that evening I was back at Bradwell towing a fourteen foot log of ten-inch-by-three deal from the Barrow Deep. My pictures of the tall mast and a little of the superstructure protruding from a smooth sea show a marked contrast to the shots in Thursday's papers of waves sweeping right over the vessel.

Much can be learnt from the traditional sailing boats of the area. For carrying cargo the Thames Spiritsail barges outlasted all other types of vessel. She was flat bottomed with lee-boards to give a clear space in the hold and rigged with an inefficient rig but one that could be handled by a small crew; two men and boy in fact. Her shoal draft, only six feet for an eighty foot vessel when laden, enabled her to reach far inland at high water and dry safely on any level bottom. Her lack of windward efficiency mattered little for she made no effort to beat against the tide but, with the *help* of the tides and a ready anchor as soon as they turned foul, reached every corner of the area. Other craft treated barges with scorn for they couldn't reef down and storm along to windward in heavy weather like a real sailing boat. A barge was said to be like an old woman; all she could do when it came on to blow was to pick up her skirts and run for shelter. In practice the barge trips were short enough to enable them to pick their weather, and if they did have to run for shelter there was shelter aplenty within the Thames Estuary into which to run. That same shelter is still there for today's weekend sailors.

The fishing smacks, on the other hand, had no problems with crew to handle the sails, for large crews were needed to handle the nets once they reached the fishing grounds. A fast trip home to market was essential, for if it took too long the fish went bad and had to be sold for a pittance as farm manure. Time spent getting out to the fishing area and returning was time wasted. Thus they developed the gaff cutter rig with topsails and other kites to keep them moving in light airs. They were not particularly shallow craft for they needed a good grip on the water when fishing and riding out bad weather.

The smack's mast was stepped on the keel but all barges had lowering masts to enable them to get up river beyond the bridges. Sail areas were large so that both types could make useful progress in light airs but on the other hand, when it did come on to blow, both could reduce sail quickly. The barge got in her topsail quickly to save her fragile topmast and brailed up part of her mainsail. Smacks reefed the mainsail, changed down to smaller headsails and, if needs be, to storm trysail and spitfire jib.

All manner of yachts sail these waters but those drawing six feet or more tend to keep to the deep water areas and harbours with deep water berths. It is perfectly possible to reach most places with boats drawing six feet but they never seem to do so, presumably because of the fear of being left high and dry after running aground. More than one laden barge leaving a narrow creek touched her bows on the shallows. Before she could struggle free the ebb swung her stern across the creek onto the opposite bank, leaving her unsupported amidships once the tide left so that she broke her back. To avoid this sort of problem barges employed a local pilot known as a huffer who also added a bit of muscle when necessary. There are many centreboard boats whose plate stows in the keel rather than intrudes in the cabin. This enables them to sail in shallow water, but they loose the advantage of being able to dry out level enough to live on board. Bilge keels or twin keels as they are sometimes known, provide something of a compromise and have sold in thousands over the last twenty-five years, but they lack the performance of keel or centreboard boats. The small centreboarder can draw as little as twelve inches with the plate up and this makes it easy for her to find a drying mooring and leave it early on the returning flood tide. Many marinas have a drying sill at the entrance. The centreboard boat will be first in every time. Much more important to my sort of sailing, she can dry out in all manner of creeks and quiet places, away from the maddening crowd.

Winds generally are light in the Thames Estuary. I can only express an opinion but I would guess that we have fewer gale warnings than any other area around the United Kingdom. Figures to hand suggest that if we concentrate the sailing season into one hour, there would be two or three minutes of flat calm, thirty minutes with winds force one to three, twenty minutes force four to five and one and a half minutes force six to seven with a little force eight. The predominance of light winds becomes even greater when we allow the yachtsman the option of staying at home when strong winds are forecast. Thus we need plenty of sail in this area, particularly when running downwind with a fair tide.

Imagine a boat running down the edge of the Maplin Sands with a fair tide of two knots in a wind force 2/3 i.e. about seven knots. The tide will be carrying her away from the wind at two knots so the effective wind is reduced to five knots. If she is making three knots through the water the wind reaches her sails at just two knots. She therefore needs a lot of sail to achieve that three knots down wind. It has either got to be gaff rig with all the kites, or Bermudian rig with a balloon spinnaker. Six hours later the same vessel returning will have the tide helping her into the wind, which makes the effective wind speed nine knots. If she is making good two knots to windward this increases the apparent wind speed to eleven knots. This is why shirt sleeved crews enjoying downwind sailing reach for a sweater as soon as they come round onto the wind, remarking that it has suddenly turned chilly. In fact windward performance is far less important to the cruising man than is often thought. If the worst comes to the worst you can always use an engine to help you to windward and leave the fumes astern. If you use an engine downwind the fumes overtake the vessel and envelop the whole boat to produce the nearest the sailor can get to the delights of being stuck in a traffic jam.

Of course a certain level of performance is necessary. I have ten miles to travel to the river mouth and another forty will take me to most of the Thames Estuary. Thus a weekend capability of one hundred miles is the passport to unlimited enjoyment of this wonderful area.

From high water on Friday evening to high water on Sunday evening is about fifty hours. If I can find one knot of tide to help me on my way and average two knots through the water, this distance can be covered in just over thirty hours which leaves some seventeen or eighteen hours for eating, sleeping or just lazing about. Drying moorings tend to be cheaper than those with water at all states of the tide, and thus the inevitable choice for many small boat owners. Alternate weeks my mooring is dry when I arrive on Friday evening and I cannot leave until sometime between three hours before and three hours after the next high water. With a fair wind I can leave as soon as she floats and sail over the flood but it is little use beating against it. Thus the time of the tides may well reduce the weekend to thirty-six hours, unless I get back very late on Sunday, but there are plenty of interesting sixty or seventy mile trips to be made.

Therefore I need a boat capable of covering one hundred miles in a weekend and shallow enough to enable me to explore the heads of creeks and rivers, wherever men traded under sail in years long gone. She must have a good performance in light airs to enable me to sail round the outer sand banks in fine weather and sturdy enough to get me out of trouble when it blows up suddenly. One last item: she must be weatherly enough to beat the length of the Wallet Channel between Harwich and the River Colne on one flood tide.

For over thirty-four years the sixteen toot gaff cutter *Shoal Waters* has fulfilled these requirements. Her best weekend trip was from Heybridge to The Oaks on the River Alde above Aldeburgh, and back, in twenty-five hours and forty minutes, a trip of over one hundred miles with four hours for sleep and twenty minutes for breakfast. Of course most weekends we sail a lot less, often going no further than the river mouth, but at least we know that, thanks to her superb suitability for this area, we have a free choice.

Chapter Three

Shoal Waters, the Hull

Sixteen years cruising in my old half-decker *Zephyr* taught me that one could live with some degree of comfort in a boat sixteen foot long, and that some very good passages *and* some very poor ones could be made. Over the years she took me north about as far as the Wash, and south as far as Poole harbour. She scared me as I have never been scared before or since, and delighted me so that I had to restrain myself from singing at the top of my voice as she danced over the waves because I found that my throat was becoming sore. Above all, she taught me to sail and understand small boats, how to woo the fickle winds, to rely on the faithful tides and to meet the sea in its many moods. Early in 1962 I decided to put an iron bar across the hull level with the mast to prevent the hull working so much when sailed hard. As I toiled knee deep in the mud, an old chap spoke to me from the sea wall and commented on the 'goo' in which I was standing. I explained that at least it was kind to her hull which was probably as old as I was. He took his pipe from his mouth, spat over the sea wall and said, 'Old as you are lad! She's as old as the two of us put together.' Later that season I conceived the idea of stepping her gear into a new hull, and quickly settled on the *Fairey Falcon*, although we continued to examine the market until the 1963 Boat Show. Other contenders were the *Silhouette* which was selling like mad at that time and available as a kit at two hundred pounds, the *Wavecrest*, the *Yachting Monthly Senior* and the *Lysander*. My experience in 1951 of fitting a tiny lifting cabin top to *Zephyr* had shown me the speed with which a gross of one inch size eight brass screws vanish into woodwork (they cost eight shillings and sixpence in those days) and I resolved that in future my limited funds must always be put into a sound hull.

I love clinker planking, its link with our Viking ancestors and its strength, but years of bailing *Zephyr* and the resulting fatigue made me yearn for a tight hull. Even a spoonful of water in a shallow hull will run from side to side as the boat heels, and soak everything once the going gets rough. Perhaps the deciding factor was that she had to be a centreboarder. The long slot in the keel weakens the whole structure and the strain causes leaks in planked hulls, especially along the garboard strake, the one adjacent to the keel. A monohull, i.e. a hull made in one piece, supports the keel instead of weakening it. The great advantage of the *Falcon* hull was that it was made of four thicknesses of agba veneer laid diagonally and hot moulded with no concessions to saving weight. Her bigger sister, the twenty-six foot *Atalanta* hull was the same thickness. In thirty-four years and nearly sixty thousand miles of cruising. I have never fitted a bilge pump. Any water that gets in is removed with a sponge.

The hull for *Shoal Waters* was ordered at the Boat Show in 1963 and delivered on the first Saturday of February during that bitterly cold winter. Odds and ends of sketches were made but I am no draughtsman and it was clear that she would have to be built on the basis that what looks right is right. Fortunately I had a fine workshop in a brick shed built originally to hold the farm charging plant in the days before mains electricity reached rural areas. I ordered two standard eight-by-four feet sheets of marine ply, one a quarter and the other three eighths of an inch thick, just to see what they were like, together with a hundred feet of one inch square mahogany. After that it was a matter of deciding what I needed, ordering it, and waiting for delivery. Gripfast nails, brass screws and Aerofix glue were used for all fixings with Mendix to fill in the gaps left by my lack of carpentry skills. Before starting I had attended the old 'Build Yourself a Dinghy' exhibition, held, I believe, at Chelsea Barracks (the forerunner of today's National Dinghy Exhibition) and I remembered a chap explaining that the days of the tongued joint were over. Just butt two pieces of wood together, glue and nail a piece of ply across the angle and you have a strong joint. Clodhopper carpentry had arrived just in time.

Fitting a shallow keel below the moulded hull to protect it when grounding or hauled ashore, for the winter, was the first problem. Shaping a solid piece of wood was beyond my skill so I used two pieces of wood three inches by a half inch, laid each side of the keel ridge and glued and fixed into the hull laminates and hog with alternate gripfast nails and brass screws every three inches. The gunwale came next. I sandwiched the laminate of agba veneer between one inch square on the inside and one and a half by half inch on the outside. The decks laid over this gave an end seal to the veneers of the hull and the rubbing strake was later put onto the gunwale rather than onto the hull so that it could be renewed when damaged without interfering with the precious laminate of the hull.

An examination of the ply soon convinced me that I should use three eighth ply throughout and keep the quarter inch sheet for the cabin top. Starting inside the hull was a daunting task but a start had to be made somewhere and the support for the plate case seemed to be the first task. When sold as a half-decked boat, this support is provided by the centre thwart. I made a bulkhead each side of the case just in front of the pivot bolt and the same height as the case. Three eighth ply was cut to shape and a series of one or two inch long pieces of one inch square mahogany were glued along the rounded edge where it joined the hull. When dry the lot was smoothed off, covered liberally with Mendex and pressed against the hull. No screws or nails went through the skin of the hull.

The bridge deck was cut one foot wide and fixed to blocks screwed into the hull so that the cabin bulkhead was six feet from the transom. At first I expected to sleep two adults in quarter berths and two children forward. The bridge deck was set three inches higher than the cockpit seats to give a little more knee room and supported aft by a piece of three-by-one which strengthened the whole fitting. Additional support to the after end of the plate case was made with two and a quarter by one and a quarter mahogany. By this time I had met a man chopping up a billiard table for firewood!

As I was using three eighth ply, no frame had to be built and skinned. The one inch square mahogany merely served to join adjacent sheets of ply. The foredeck and side decks were glued to the gunwale. Then the side decks were trimmed off nine inches wide, and one inch square was fitted along the inner edge to take the cabin sides. The cabin sides were carried six inches into the cabin to make a sort of box girder round the cabin and provide some useful lockers for small items. Cabin beams were a problem, for even beams of modest curvature had to be cut from a deep expensive piece of wood. I solved this by using wood one inch deeper than the finished beam, cutting the curve and glueing the offcuts from the top back on the bottom. With a backing of ply offcuts this solved the problem economically. A piece of oak from an barn provided the Samson post, and that completed the work on the cabin since no money was available for floorboards etc.

A deep comfortable cockpit was made much along the lines of the *Zephyr*'s with the coamings the same height above the seats as the arms of my favourite armchair at home for maximum comfort at the helm and a clear view forward over the cabin top for safety underway. Perhaps the most comfortable seat is that for the crew, facing forwards sitting on the bridge deck with feet in the cabin and elbows resting on the cabin top while using binoculars. A nine inch wide afterdeck was made to give a locker underneath and to provide the helmsman with a feeling of security from the sea astern, so lacking in those craft with just a bare transom.

A toe rail, one and a half inches high runs round the edge of, and at right angles to, the deck and the decks themselves had sand sprinkled on the wet undercoat before the topcoat to give a superb non-slip effect. I bought two packets of International deck sand at one shilling and sixpence a packet, and one friend at the club scornfully worked out how much I was paying a ton for 'just sand', but it lasted for over twenty-five years. It must be the cheapest form of safety on the market.

The fisherman anchor stows neatly on the foredeck with the crown over the bows, and the chain is collected in a plastic bucket jammed forward of the Samson post. For the first season I used the rudder off *Zephyr* but was able to make a drop rudder to the pattern sold with the completed hull the following year. It took less paint for the hull than I expected, but pint after pint of varnish vanished into the woodwork. The week before Whitsun all was ready and the great moment came. The rigging made at Heybridge Basin chandlers fitted perfectly and within a few minutes I realised that I had a winner on my hands. As usual the wind blew hard from the east at Whitsun and I sheltered with my two eldest children in Lawling Creek, unwilling to endanger them in an untried boat. The next weekend came in cold and dull with wind from the north. I left on the Friday evening tide, sailed to the Crouch as the sun set and passed out through Havengore next morning to reach the Medway by lunchtime. Then I sailed back round the Whittaker to Fambridge and home on Sunday via the Spitway. *Shoal Waters* had completed her first one ton trip.

For the first year I painted the whole hull green and left it so that the weed would grow on the hull to give me a waterline. Soon after launching I did a rudimentary stability test with her on her mooring by standing in the water and pulling down on the peak halyard until the boat was horizontal. I let go and she came upright instantly. Of course the plate was up for the water was only three feet deep. By August I had recast the lead ballast from *Zephyr*, and put it inside *Shoal Waters*. Without antifoulant the weed and barnacles grew quickly. In order to scrub the bottom I anchored the boat in three feet of water and asked my wife to heave down on the halyard to career the hull. She was unable to get the boat over far enough for my liking so I handed her the brush and tried the halyard myself. To my delight, when the boat came over at forty-five degrees my feet came off the bottom and I swung in towards the ship. Stability was not going to be a problem. People are so concerned with buoyancy for when they capsize that they have forgotten the stabilising effect of ballast to prevent a capsize. I have since tried some stiff tests under sail over shallow water where a sunken hull could be recovered at low tide, and she just doesn't go over enough to get water in over the coamings. Of course she could capsize on the face of a large steep wave, if I ever went out in such conditions, but the fact is that I do not. When asked about buoyancy I delight in explaining that I carry psychological buoyancy: two hundred and eighty pounds of lead. It doesn't prevent my capsizing once but at least I know it cannot happen twice and the knowledge that a capsize means drowning tends to put one off the idea altogether.

At first foam cushions for the bunks were out of the question but a feather bed failed to get a bid at the village jumble sale and I got it for sixpence. The feathers restowed in plastic fertiliser bags served for several years.

Now we have two cushioned bunks forward of the centreboard bulkhead, a galley aft on the port side and a seat which lifts to provide a third bunk on the starboard quarter. It will never be a roomy boat but at least it is warm, dry and very comfortable.

Chapter Four

Shoal Waters, the Rig

Once the hull of a boat has been completed it is unlikely to be changed during the life of the vessel. Alterations can be made. The famous false counter stern on the *Dulcibella* in 'Riddle of the Sands' is one instance and records show that many old fishing boats were cut in half and lengthened, but it must have been an expensive game and called for skills hard to find today. On the other hand, changing the rig is simple, not much more than the cost of a new mast and mainsail. Few old sailing boats wore the same sail plan throughout their reign.

The sixteen foot half-decker *Zephyr* was gunter rigged when I bought her in 1948, and even then bare ends to the yard and boom showed that the mainsail had been reduced by one vertical cloth. She sailed well, far better than *Shoal Waters* when going to windward through the sort of lop we get with strong winds against the tide in shallow water, but my, she was wet! I sailed her hard from her moorings at Maldon, visiting most corners of the Thames Estuary, the Norfolk Broads and the Wash. The one thing that I came to dread was lowering the long yard in a following wind and sea in order to run under headsail only. It invariably went into the water and had to be hauled back on board dripping wet. Of course I didn't know about the age old double topping lift or lazy jacks as they are known in larger vessels when rigged in a more elaborate manner. Like all good seamanlike measures it is simple. A line leads from the hounds down to the boom one third in from the after end, through an eye, back to hounds on the other side of the mast and down to the deck where it is made fast. It is set up hard before lowering the mainsail, firstly to take up the weight of the boom the same as the standard topping lift, but as a bonus, to provide a guide that must result in the yard (or gaff) coming down on top of the boom together with the sail completely under control.

After three years I cut the throat out of the gunter mainsail to give a long, straight luff, fixed part of the yard on top of the mast and went Bermudian to visit the south coast as far as Poole harbour, and have another look at the Broads. By 1957 a steady job, a wife and a growing family cut sailing to a minimum. Time and money were tight. An attempt to give up sailing failed after a couple of days on the beach at Clacton and Felixstowe. A new mainsail was needed but there was no question of ordering one from a sailmaker. Joy bought me a length of unbleached calico for my birthday and I set out to make a mainsail, with her help on the sewing machine.

There was plenty of sailing available on larger craft and on one of them I came across the first Terylene mainsail made by a firm of West Mersea sailmakers. The quality was such that we preferred to use the old cotton one. I realised that a bad Bermudian mainsail was a dead loss, but a gaff one could always be pulled into some sort of shape by the extra adjustments possible to a four sided sail. Nowadays sailmakers have realised this and introduced further adjustments, such as Cunningham holes, bendy masts and adjustable backstays to improve Bermudian sails. *Zephyr* put to sea in 1957 with her new gaff rig and I loved it. She performed well enough but above all, I just liked the look of it. This is how we choose our wives, which works out well for most of us and the same system over hundreds of years of farming has made British livestock the envy of the world. Six years later *Shoal Waters* set out on her maiden voyage with the gear from *Zephyr*, in the hope that funds would be available to buy a new suit of sails at the end of the first season. In fact I was glad of the chance to test it out before taking a hard and fast decision. I never considered the idea of making a Terylene mainsail. The basic material costs so much and lasts so many years that it is well worth paying to have it made properly. I have no doubt that if I made ten sails I could get a useful one, but once every fifteen years is no way to master such an important and historic art. I was tempted to go Bermudian as the *Falcon* is sold with the same rig as the *Albacore* dinghies raced at the club and second hand sails were going cheap.

At this time there were few gaff boats about and those one did see were not very inspiring examples of the breed. Unknown to me as I built *Shoal Waters* during the long cold winter of 1963, a small group of enthusiasts were organising the first East Coast Old Gaffers race for July of that year (cutting out all yachting magazines was one of the economies that gathered the money to build her). They hoped for twelve entries and got thirty, including the month old *Shoal Waters*. Most of the entries were sorry old things but a hint of a golden future was there in the glorious sight of *Corista*, a thirteen year old forty foot gaff cutter with over forty Channel and North Sea crossings to her credit. I can still visualise the stirring sight of her as she overtook me off Thirslet Spit once the wind came up on the nose (we had got ahead over the last of the flood by

Comparison of progress in windward made by Bermudian and gaff rigged yachts when beating.

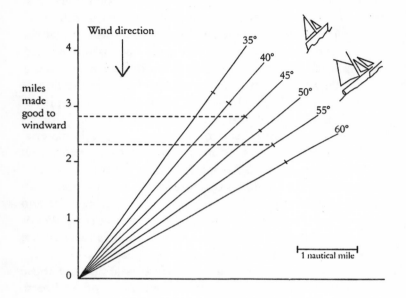

Analysis with Bermudian sailing at 45° and gaff at 55° to wind

Tide		Speed made good to windward		Advantage of Bermudian rig
Fair	Foul	Gaff	Bermudian	
Nil	Nil	2.2 kts	2.8 kts	27%
–	1 kt	1.2	1.8	50%
–	2 kts	0.2	0.8	300%
1 kt	–	3.2	3.8	19%
2 kts	–	4.2	4.8	14%

creeping along the shore). This was my kind of sailing! The contrast next day as I ran back into the River Blackwater to meet the dreary stream of Bermudian nonentities probably settled the matter but one final test killed all doubts. At the start of the three day August bank holiday break the wind came in from the north-east and *Shoal Waters* beat up the coast to the River Ore. Next morning the wind went south-west, making it a beat home which she completed together with a visit to Walton Backwaters. That was all the performance that I needed.

Thirty years later I no longer have to apologise for my old-fashioned rig. New gaff vessels are advertised in the yachting press and on view at the Boat Show. The Old Gaffers Race on the Blackwater each July is now a festival of the sailmaker's art with over half the craft sporting topsails. With a start downwind it is a sight that has to be seen to be believed, for none of the usual restrictions on racing sails apply. If you can find somewhere to hang it, up it goes. A Dutchman who presented the prizes some years ago summed it up when he said. 'Neffer haff I seen boats mit so much sails!' He had hit the nail right on the head. The great advantage of gaff rig is the large area of sail that can be carried downwind without resorting to balloon spinnakers or big boys. The racing man's obsession with windward performance does not apply to cruising.

Look at it this way. The diagram opposite shows a yacht close hauled on the port tack making four knots through the water. The courses show the progress of boats sailing forty, forty-five, fifty, fifty-five degrees off the wind, their position after one hour's sailing at four knots and horizontal lines transferring these positions to the scale so that speed made good to windward can be read off. Exactly how high a boat points, including allowance for leeway, can be argued from now to doomsday, but let us assume that the Bermudian cruiser points forty-five degrees off the wind and makes good 2.8 knots while the gaffer sags fifty-five degrees off the wind and only makes good 2.2 knots. This is a superiority of twenty-seven percent for the Bermudian boat. Apply one knot or foul tide to each vessel and the speeds made good over the bottom drop to 1.8 and 1.2 knots, a superiority of fifty percent. Increase the tide to two knots and the relative speeds become 0.8 and 0.2 knots, giving the Bermudian boat a superiority of three hundred percent.

Now let me confess that I am a retired civil servant, a career in which everything has to be proved by statistics and a certain amount of, perhaps not cooking, but certainly slight warming up to get the right result is not unknown. Nevertheless, what I have shown does happen in practice. A foul tide will sort out the boats with poor windward performance. No one likes being passed on the water and it can be a miserable business for the owner of the slower boat. Perhaps the worst cases occur on the Norfolk Broads when the Bermudian boat can just fetch a reach of a winding, narrow river, round a bend to leeward, and scorch off with a beam wind while the gaffer has to make a tack at right angles to the river across a foul tide with all the dismay and delay that that entails. All is not gloom. Give the boats a fair tide of one knot and the speeds made good become 3.8 and 3.2 knots, only nineteen percent better for the triangular sail, and if the fair tide is two knots the speeds made good over the bottom become 4.8 and 4.2 knots, just fourteen percent better. This is still a substantial advantage and only tolerable if gaff rig will make up this deficiency to windward off the wind. A glance at the compass and the wind direction will show that nearly three quarters of the time you spend sailing will be off the wind. Thus, if we think of the case of the gaffer beating with a fair tide of one knot with a performance twenty per cent less than the Bermudian boat, it has got to be at least ten per cent better on all other points of sailing. I am pleased to inform you that she will be.

A word of warning here. There is nothing magic about having a bit of wood at the top of the mainsail. Gaff rig is purely and simply a way of hoisting more sail on a given boat. It becomes particularly important as the man who goes to sea for fun tends to sail most in light weather and stops home in hard winds. Some of the modern Boat Show gaffers look to me like Bermudian boats with a slit across the mainsail to take the gaff. Even the topsail does not extend beyond the top of the mast. You cannot have a standing backstay with gaff rig so the boom may as well extend well over the sternpost to give a large sail area. Several of our old gaffers have booms longer than their waterline length. A yard will carry the topsail well above the mast head to give more sail area where the wind blows strongest. The gaffer with a short boom may suit the proud owner, but it will not give the performance off the wind to make up the loss of performance to windward.

Few people have experience of both types of rig on the same boat, but I met one recently. He lost his gaff rig together with topsail over the bows in the Yare Navigation Race and decided to take the opportunity to go Bermudian. In spite of cutting a hundred square feet from the mainsail, he was surprised to find that he had to add another three and a half hundred weight of ballast to the keel to restore her original stiffness, which seems to answer the criticism that gaff rig has too much weight aloft. I suspect that the explanation has much to do with the tendency of the gaff to sag to leeward. This is normally quoted as a deficiency of the rig; usually by people who have never used it. In practice, this is a major safety factor, for as the boat heels to a squall, the sagging gaff lets much of the force of the wind escape harmlessly over the top. In the same situation a Bermudian-rigged craft with a kicking strap holding the mainsail flat can only relieve the pressure of the wind by heeling over even further.

The point that I have tried so laboriously to make is that if you are going to spend a lot of time beating over the tide, go Bermudian. If you can so order your affairs as to normally work a fair tide to windward, gaff rig will serve you better. Of course the racing man wants windward performance because he must sail the course set by the race officer. This will often include a beat over the tide. I recall enjoying a drink aboard a certain royal yacht some years ago during a well known early August regatta and listening to the owner's husband, a man known for his forthright opinions, expressing the view after a day in which few boats crossed the finishing line (himself included) that the race organisers never consulted either a tide table or a weather forecast. Things get worse as you go down the racing ladder. On the other hand, the cruising man will take a fair tide as naturally as he selects the up or down escalator at the underground station depending on whether he wants to go up or down.

At the end of the 1963 season I took *Shoal Waters* round to Arthur Taylor's sail loft just above the quay at Maldon, and in time honoured fashion we 'measured the hole'. Then we went into his little office and he drew out the existing sail plan which we adjusted to give a bigger sail area that 'looked right'. Fifteen years and twenty-five thousand miles later I had no hesitation in ordering the same again (apart from making each of the two reefs six inches deeper). The sail was made loose-footed which enables me to adjust the flow to suit the wind, flat when it blows hard and curved for light airs. It is accepted as important for headsails, why not for mainsails?

The next problem was whether to step the mast on the keel or on deck. I like the idea of a mast passing through the deck and stepped on the keel so that it is capable of standing up on its own, merely supported by the rigging. On the other hand, a lowering mast is the passport to many delightful areas above bridges so that in spite of the danger of loosing the mast over the side with a simple rigging failure, it was the inevitable choice. The foot of the mast fits into a gunmetal tabernacle (luxury, sheer unashamed luxury) so that it pivots on a bolt when lowering. A deck-stepped mast with no pivot loses the advantage of easy lowering, as there is nothing to control the foot as it comes down. I never fit the second tabernacle bolt when the mast is set up and only use four deck bolts instead of the six for which there are holes in their casting. The reason is that if the rigging goes the mast will fall anyway and it is better to rip the bolts out from the plywood deck than damage the tabernacle beyond repair.[2]

At first *Shoal Waters* was sloop-rigged with a very short bowsprit, but I knew that if it carried away the mast would come down as the fore-stay leads to the bowsprit end. When I changed to cutter rig I was delighted to fix the fore-stay to the stemhead fitting (see fig. 2) and sail happy in the knowledge that a broken bowsprit would not be a calamity!

---

[2]In May 1997 while *Shoal Waters* was on a trailer the mast hit an obstruction and ripped the tabernacle out of the foredeck. It was quickly and easily repaired.

Apart from the advantages of the extra sail and the picturesque appearance, the fitting of a bowsprit to a small yacht brings more safety than many of the expensive gimmicks pumped onto the market these days under that broad title. The bowsprit requires a bobstay to support it leading from the stem at the waterline. It is a route back on board for a man in the water, something that becomes increasingly important as topsides rise ever higher. I always tell my evening classes before the Boat Show comes along to imagine that they are in the water with their chin level with the waterline of the boat that they are thinking of buying.

'How will you get back on board?' or even, 'is there anything you can reach to hang on to?'

Our bobstay saved a chap's life in 1979. It was the sort of thing that could happen to anyone. There he was in the middle of the River Yare below Reedham with a rope around his waist which he couldn't untie and a fifty-six pound weight at the other end on the bottom while a strong ebb tide threatened to drag him under. Apparently the motor cruiser got stuck and in pulling it clear, another boat left one of its ropes round the propeller before departing. The cruiser was one of the floating tea tray variety and drifted downstream fast. The only ropes they have are a mooring rope, bow and stern, and a rope on the mud weight, which is used in this area instead of an anchor. He tied the mooring ropes together, fixed one end round his waist and tried to swim ashore. It is always further than it looks so they added the rope from the mud weight to give him a little more scope. It is spliced to the weight so they had to untie it from the cleat on the foredeck. As he still couldn't reach the shore they decided to anchor and dropped the weight over the side! We came round the bend as he was complaining of being dragged through the water (by the tide) and in broad northern accents his mates replied.

'Don't be daft. You are stood still. We are the ones who are moving.' Joy and I roared with laughter as we unravelled the story but soon began to beat back over the tide as the seriousness of the situation dawned on us. Then the man in the water began to call for help and told us he could not untie the rope around his waist. This was one time when I could have appreciated a little more windward ability, but a lucky slant enabled us to shoot along the lee shore before tacking across so that he could grasp the bobstay. Yes! bobstays can be life-savers.

Both headsails are set on the good old-fashioned but simple and reliable Whykham Martin furling gear. It is rarely advertised for it was never patented when it was invented at the turn of the century, but it is available if you search around. Once you have the upper and lower fittings any headsail can be set between them. I have three staysails; the smallest a spitfire jib just twelve square feet. The fittings revolve on normal bicycle ball bearings packed with grease. The lower one picks up salt water and needs repacking every two or three years, but the top one seems to go on for ever. The sails must be specially made by a sailmaker who understands these things and I cannot over stress the advantages of going to your local loft. Apart from making new sails, he will keep the patterns until you want to reorder and will always help out with repairs in a hurry when needs be. Sails are so important that the slight extra cost of personal service is money well spent, as opposed to chasing discounts and other enticements offered by those sailmakers who have to take expensive advertising in the yachting press to stay busy. The only thing that can go wrong with this gear is for the furling line to tangle round the outside of the drum assembly so that the sail will not furl. Always let the line run out though your fingers as you pull the sheet to set the sail and make fast afterwards with just enough slack so that the sail sets freely, but not enough slack to tangle round the drum.

I use gunmetal snap shackles at head, tack and clew for my headsails, although this is generally frowned upon. I find they serve me well and it makes changing sails easy and quick. It wasn't until I became a judge in a 'one of a kind' rally that I realised the snags. One boat fitted with snap shackles hoisted the headsails and let them flutter in a force five breeze for ten or fifteen minutes and the sheets came adrift several times. With furling gear the sail stays rolled up until it is needed, so that it never need be left fluttering which saves wear and tear on sails and the nerves of the crew.

The Whykham Martin gear is only for furling not reefing, although with the cutter rig the furling of one sail halves the sail area forward of the mast. These days there are a number of roller reefing gears on the market for headsails and the owners seem satisfied with them. I don't like them for the strain on the drum and line, when a sail is used half-rolled, must be considerable. One flaw in any part of the fitting or the breaking of the line and the lot could suddenly unroll in a gale. The problems of tackling such a rogue sail in rough weather defy imagination, particularly in the dark. It may happen only once in a lifetime but that would be once too much for me. Changing furled sails is so easy. No flogging mass of stiff wet sailcloth to fight on a heaving foredeck, just one docile sausage to change for a smaller one while the boat looks after herself under mainsail only. Of course the headsail roller reefing gear may suit the chap who sticks to sheltered water.

In really light airs I use a ghoster of nylon that doubles as a balloon jib and an old-fashioned spinnaker setting on the opposite side to the mainsail. It sets from the masthead to the end of the bowsprit and overlaps the main. It has just one sheet which is often led to the end of the main boom, a practice banned by racing folk and therefore well worth looking at by the cruising man. With the wind aft the tack can be brought back to the foot of the mast and the sail boomed out with the sounding pole. Of course it means that I cannot sound, but one should not be carrying such a sail if in danger of running aground. This sail is strictly for very light airs, often with no apparent wind at all and does sterling service but is taken in the moment the wind makes up its mind and settles down to become a working breeze.

The topsail came late, in fact the first one was made out of an old *Albacore* jib given to me by a fellow club member. It was only intended as a bit of fun but I soon realised that it was earning its keep, for that is where the wind is. Wind speed increases rapidly as you go up the mast. Incidentally the forecast speed is for the wind thirty feet above sea level. A year later I had a proper topsail made up. At first we lashed it to the bamboo yard each time we wanted to use it but now it is a working sail which is used much of the time and stays lashed on the yard all season. The lot stows in the cabin port side above the bunk. I rigged it in traditional style with a bowline to the peak as a sheet and a downhaul, but I have become lazy over the years and now merely tie the tack and clew to the boom so that I only have the halyard to contend with in use. This can be let fly in a squall or for low bridges, but of course the whole mainsail must be lowered to take in the sail when it pipes up. A word of warning for anyone thinking of fitting a topsail for the first time. It is difficult to get it to set well at first and the problems will occupy you at the helm for the first few weeks, quite apart from the urge to just look up and admire it. There is a very real danger of ramming another craft either under way or even on a mooring. I had several near scrapes. Perhaps the best comment on topsails was made by the late Francis B. Cooke who sailed the east coast from the 1890s until after the Second World War: 'Men cursed them and swore that they would have done with them. Then they went to their sailmakers and ordered larger ones. Topsails, the glory of gaff rig.'

So much for the lazy days of 'topsail weather'. A rising wind calls for an altogether more urgent and businesslike attitude. There are two rows of reef points on the mainsail and the reef pendants and tack lashings are in place at all times. With the original mainsail the eighteen inch reefs did not reduce the sail area sufficiently and I found in practice that the first reef made so little difference that it was not worth putting in. I either used full sail or two reefs. When I had the second sail made each reef was made six inches deeper and this seems to be about right. The first reef reduces the mainsail by twenty per cent and, used with the staysail, gives a well-balanced rig once the wind gets too much for full working sail. In crowded harbours and anchorages, I furl the staysail and use the jib instead as it gives better visibility for the helmsman. The second reef, which is a foot deeper than the reef in the old sail, takes out another twenty per cent, giving a total reduction of forty per cent, and makes life comfortable when things begin to get really lively. It can be used with either the staysail or the tiny spitfire jib.

It will be apparent from the above details that I stick firmly to the good old-fashioned tradition of keeping the balance of the sail plan when reducing sail. Not for me this modern fad of headsail only, mainsail only or worse still, reefing the main and retaining a large headsail. A tiny headsail has two great virtues. Firstly it can be used aback to knock the boat's head round when tacking into the sort of short fussy waves one meets when beating with the tide. Secondly, in a sudden squall, the main can be eased a little and the headsail sheeted in hard so that it drives the wind off the leach into the luff of the mainsail; causing it to lift and thus in effect, reducing the working area of that sail until the squall has passed.

At the top of force five rising six my trysail comes out from its hiding place starboard side, right forward under the foredeck where it is always bent onto its own small gaff ready at all times (see fig. 3). It is strongly made, five feet at the head; six in the hoist and seven in the foot to give about forty-five square feet and thirty when reefed. To set it the mainsail comes down and is firmly lashed into the scissors type boom crutch. The main sheet and the topping lift are stowed out of the way and the trysail is brought out and laid along the boom. The jaws are lashed in place round the mast and the peak and throat halyards transferred from the mainsail to the trysail. The tack is made fast to the gooseneck at the spider-band with a lashing permanently in place on the trysail and the gaff hoisted hard up. At this time the trysail is brailed up to the throat and the rest controlled by the tack line marlin hitched round it hammock fashion. The brailing line is released and led down to the topping lift fairlead on the forward end of the cabin top and aft to the topping lift cleat handy for the cockpit. The luff line is unhitched from the sail and laced round the mast. The trysail sheet is middled and temporarily half-hitched to the tiller, while each end is led over a clam cleat, through a fairlead up to one side of the double block on the clew of the sail and back to an eye on the quarter. A piece of shock cord is used to hold the skirt of the sail to the mast.

To get underway, take off the shock cord, release the brailing line and heave out the sheet on the lee side. Having two sheets makes the trysail a bit of a handful at first. Unfurl the spitfire jib and you are underway, fit for the yachtsman's summer gale. As well as getting out of a mess, this rig can be used in smooth sheltered water to give a little sailing on those days when other craft stay on their moorings, and racing dinghies that venture down the ramp capsize within minutes. Observers always come up with the same comment. 'You look comfortable,' which seems to me to sum up this essential sail.

Now all these sails must be controlled from the cockpit where the layout is crucial. The mainsheet is a single whip because this uses less rope (which saves money) and minimises the total of gash rope under my feet in the cockpit. It leads from the horse on the afterdeck, through two blocks along the boom to a cam cleat in the centre of the bridge deck. Thus the tail of the sheet is handy to my knee for instant release to ease the sail in a sudden squall. Most important, a single whip mainsheet runs out much quicker than a multiple purchase. It is harder to get the sail in but I can always luff up a little or reach up and get a purchase by swigging down on the sheet between the blocks on the boom.

The hoist for the centreboard is a fourfold purchase with the tail in a clam cleat under the mainsheet cleat, once again handy for instant attention as soon as the plate 'whispers' to me that it is scraping the bottom.

The jib and staysail sheets lead in through the coamings just behind the cabin to a pair of clam cleats. When tacking they can be handled together with a final adjustment to each sheet as the boat gathers way on the new tack.

All sheets and the plate hoist can be handled by the helmsman sitting one side of the cockpit. When short tacking in reasonable conditions I do not need to change sides. Some years ago I tacked back and forth in this manner waiting for the bridge at Havengore to open while a Silhouette buzzed round and round in noisy circles under motor. They were impressed and made enquiries as to whom I might be.

'He just sat there as comfortable as if he was watching television!'

That's my kind of sailing!

Chapter Five

Learning the Area

Man is a land animal with an instinctive fear of the sea, however much he may love the boats in which he sails upon it. In fact sailing is a very safe sport. The most dangerous part of the weekend trip is over once you drive your car off the Queen's highway into the club car park and climb on board the boat. On an average weekend thirty or forty people will be killed on the roads before you step onto dry land again. You know that you will not be one of them, which is more than any landlubber can say. Strangely enough, most of us navigate the horrors of the highways without turning a hair but get a feeling of sheer panic as the shore drops away when we venture out to sea for the first time. It is a case of preferring the devil we know to the one we don't. The answer is quite simple: learn the way of a ship in the midst of the sea as well as you know that of a motor car on the road. Fortunately it is an easier trade because on the road you are dependent on the mistakes or misjudgements of other road users. At sea collisions are rare, particularly ones involving injury or loss of life. Any disasters that befall you will be your own fault, whether through ignorance or carelessness.

The best way to tackle ignorance is by attending your local evening classes teaching the Royal Yachting

Association's Day Skipper syllabus, and following it up with a one week practical course to qualify for the certificate. Unfortunately the RYA have not been able to negotiate an agreement with Father Neptune whereby he guarantees not to drown certificate holders. Remember that he is the ultimate examiner. Every time that you leave your mooring you will be examined by him as lightly or as thoroughly as he sees fit. If you pick up your mooring on Sunday evening you have passed. If your body is washed up on the beach a week next Thursday you have failed. The death penalty may have been abolished on shore for murdering old ladies but it is still in force over the sea wall for bad seamanship. Each year he continues to reap a harvest of unwitting novices and experienced hands who just got careless.

Few boats flounder at sea. The trouble comes inshore where land and water mix, and nowhere is the mix more intricate than in the wide triangular estuary of the River Thames between London Bridge, Orfordness and the North Foreland. Learning the area is a long job but an infinitely rewarding one, The reward is quite simply, safe sailing and plenty of it.

Study the chart by all means, read every book you can get hold of about the area, but none of it really sinks in until you are afloat and begin to feel your way out to sea. Shore marks are few, the Naze Tower, the radar towers on Foulness and the Isle of Grain power station chimney which gives us a fine mark at the entrance to the River Medway. Most of the navigation is done by reference to buoys, a few historic beacons and some massive gun towers left over from the last war. The towers and beacons are extremely useful once you know them, but they do not have names on them and can only be identified by reference to the charts. Fortunately the buoys all have names or numbers. In spite of all the clever navigation tricks taught at evening classes (including my own), most of us navigate the estuary the same way we find our way about the London underground system, identifying the buoys just as we read the station names out of the carriage window and counting them off on the map or chart until we come to the one we want. I cannot over emphasise the importance of *positive* identification. Read the whole name. Many yachtsmen are convinced that the Elder Brethren of Trinity House have devised a special method of anchoring these buoys so that no matter from which direction they are approached, the name is always on the other side! The problem of reading the names has become even more difficult with the advent of the new cardinal buoys. Not only are the names written vertically, which has made them popular with visiting Chinese yachtsmen but difficult for the natives used to reading words horizontally but they are written partly in black letters on a yellow background and partly in yellow on black!

Above all, don't *wish* the buoy that comes in sight into being the buoy you *want* it to be. This may sound fantastic to the newcomer to sailing but it is strange what the sea and fatigue can do to your senses. Some years ago a leading yachting magazine told the story of a trip to Norway on which the two-man crew had a rough time. All things, however bad, come to an end and they sighted land, identified the lighthouse, passed under the bridge they expected to find according to the chart and moored up in the expected harbour. Everything on board was soaking wet so they got a taxi to the nearest hotel to spend the night warm and dry. Next morning they hailed a taxi and asked for the harbour by name. He pointed out that it was over fifty kilometres away. They were in the wrong harbour!

The lighthouse, the bridge and the harbour had all been wrongly identified, A small boat friend of mine did an epic winter voyage some years ago up the Thames to the Oxford Canal and home via the River Nene and the Wash. On the last leg back to Burnham he mistook the Heaps buoy for the North Buxey buoy, the East Barrow beacon with a cross top-mark for the Buxey beacon with a 'T' shaped top-mark and drove up onto the East Barrow sand at high water bending his centre-plate. Fortunately the midnight tide came back as smooth as silk and he was able to continue the trip to Burnham under motor but it illustrates the dangers. I repeat: *positive identification*, even if it means another ten minutes beating to get close enough to read the name.

For a start, sail out of the mouth of the river, purely and simply to identify and familiarise yourself with the local buoys, rather than using them to guide you on a trip to some other creek or river. By all means learn the language of the buoys (Hydrographic Office publication 'Maritime Buoyage System 'A'') but for small boats the significance is of minimal importance. One can usually borrow, i.e. cut inside, the buoys laid to guide deep draft shipping from the far corners of the world. In fact you are often safer to do so as it keeps you out of the shipping lanes. The local buoyage systems are a different kettle of fish. The best way to gauge them is to think of the traffic for which they are intended. Those on the busy rivers Orwell and Medway are much the same as Trinity House buoys, for big ships use these rivers. The buoys on the Blackwater and Colne are just for coasters at the top of the tide. Many of them dry at low water. The little fellows put down by the Walton and Frinton yacht club to mark the intricate channel into the Backwaters are strictly for yachts and woe betide even a shoal draft cruiser that attempts to pass inside them anywhere near low water.

One word of warning about these local marks. They are not so reliable as Trinity House buoys. Sailing up the Blackwater in July one season, I found no sign of buoys numbers one or two. After I had moored up I took my camera and walked along the sea wall to the canal basin where I photographed them looking very smart in fresh coats of paint. I took the matter up with the local pilot who replied, 'Surely you knew when you saw that they weren't there that I was painting them!' which is fine for the locals but can make life difficult for visitors.

It is not purely the danger that local marks might not be there but worse still, they may have been dragged out of position. I remember Number Seven on the Blackwater, that guards the spit west of Ford Creek went walkabout once and ended up on the mud off the tail of Osea Island where it stayed for several weeks. Trinity House buoys are handled from special vessels designed for the job. Powerful derricks handle the massive weights and mooring chains. On the other hand, local marks may well be put out by the harbourmaster using his small launch. The weights to anchor the buoy may have to be lifted over the side by hand and this limits the size that can be used. The smaller the weight the sooner it will drag.

No yacht or fishing boat should ever tie up to a navigation buoy. Don't hesitate to report any vessel you see moored in this way, for it is just as much a danger to sailors as any seventeenth century Cornish wrecker. Over the years local buoys become firm friends, as shown by the warm murmurs of recognition that greet my colour slides of them when I talk to clubs during the winter.

The poor relation of the navigation system is the broom or withy, a long pole cut from the hedgerow, trimmed but not topped and fixed into the mud. They are usually but not always visible at high water, but some cover. The withy marks exactly what the chap who put it there intended it to mark. As they have a limited life, uncertain prospects of renewal and are easily knocked over by passing craft, they are not marked on charts, although the presence of them in a given creek may well be stated. Don't let your craft drift against them or hit them with the boom. A line of withies often indicates low water springs. A profusion of them all over a creek is a sure indication of oyster beds and there is usually a weather beaten notice somewhere, indicating 'No Mooring'. Individual withies can mean anything, from a boat that sank last month to a heap of stone for the sea wall that has lain there unused since the Thirties. The only way to sort out withies is to sail the creeks early with the young flood, before the banks cover, and see where they are. One or two hours after low water the channels are already full while the mudflats are still uncovered (see fig. 4). The actual time will vary with each locality but the water can be four, five or even six feet deep. Half an hour later the mud is covered and it is impossible for the stranger to tell whereabouts the channels run. Perhaps the best example of this is at Leigh on Sea. The first time I took *Shoal Waters* up to the old jetty on the young flood I was amazed to see the local fishing bawleys come roaring in one behind the other, their bulky hulls almost filling the channel. I have often wondered if they steer them or just let the boats find their own way between the steep sides, for no way could they mount the banks.

One river does try to be more helpful, the River Alde above Aldeburgh where the winding channel to Snape is

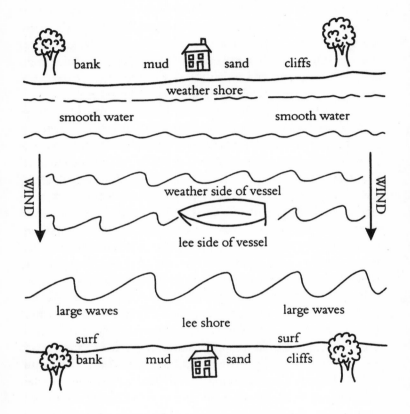

The weather and lee shores are defined relative to the vessel.

The size of the waves will depend on the height of the weather shore, the distance from that shore, the force of the wind and the length of time for which it has been blowing.

marked with withies topped by red cans (yes old bean cans painted red), to be left to port and green flags to starboard. Apart from aiding navigation, withies add immensely to the charm of the lonely creeks. They must be the oldest form of navigation marks and have a venerable, even prehistoric air about them. Bits of seaweed catch in the twigs at the top and the sun and salt air bleaches them white. Gliding along with the tide in misty moonlight as ghostly fingers tremble in the current is a never to be forgotten experience.

In spite of all these marks, sooner or later you will go aground as surely as night follows day. The important thing is to recognise where it is merely inconvenient and where it is downright dangerous. This brings us to the question of the lee shore, the *bête noire* of all seafarers. To the sailor, the lee shore is the shore on the lee side of the vessel, the shore onto which the wind is blowing. The weather shore is the shore on the weather side of the vessel, the shore from which the wind is blowing (see diagram). A small boat that goes aground will find a world of difference between the two. The water near the weather shore will be smooth even calm. A boat that touches and immediately reduces her draft by raising the centre-plate or getting the crew to heel her over (or in the case of some patterns of bilge keels, coming upright) will blow out into deeper water and safety. Even if stuck firmly on a falling tide, the boat will settle quietly and float smoothly when the tide returns (provided of course that the wind does not shift). The lee shore will have waves breaking on it. Their size will depend on the strength of the wind, how long it has been blowing and the scope of open water to windward. A boat that touches and stops becomes helpless. She won't answer to the rudder, the tiller dies in your hand and the sails, instead of driving her forward through the water, now merely serve to blow her sideways onto the shore. Any measures taken to reduce her draft will just get her more firmly on the mud. Those cheerful waves that chuckled along the hull out in the channel now become vicious and dangerous, moving horizontally in the direction of the beach. Even little waves six inches high will slam against the hull and burst over the deck and cabin top. There is a saying among land rubbers when things go wrong, 'There are worse troubles at sea', but once your ship is on a lee shore in heavy weather there just isn't any worse situation in which you could be. Over the years more sailing ships have been lost on a lee shore than any other cause. It is the one situation in which a proud vessel designed to woo the power of the wind becomes just a helpless nonentity. No lesser a book than the Londsdale Library book on yacht cruising in its advice on how to get off a lee shore councils, 'Don't get on one!' I can do no better than repeat that advice. Thus in all waters, familiar and unfamiliar, flirt as blatantly as you like with the weather shore but never go near the lee shore.

Now of course the wind will not always be on the beam. A head wind is the most useful of all for entering difficult rivers or creeks. The important thing when exploring shallow areas is to distinguish deep water from shoal, in particular, if you suddenly find yourself in shallow water, to know which way to steer to get back into deep water. To do this you must keep a check on the depth. The echo sounder is the current toy here, but it only tells you the depth if someone is watching it. More vessels go aground today than before the advent of the echo sounder because people take more risks but fail to maintain the high standard of vigilance such equipment needs. Far better for the shoal draft vessel to stick to the old-fashioned sounding pole. With a light cane eight or ten feet long, I can sound my way along the edge of a bank for miles, swinging it as easily as a walker uses a walking stick. This system never works better than when beating into a strange creek (or a known one at night or in fog). As soon as the cane touches the mud, say five or six feet, slap the helm over and the little vessel comes round onto the other tack and heads for deep water. It is one case afloat in which you cannot go wrong. Perhaps the classic example is the Whittaker Channel which runs south-west from the Swin between the Buxey and Foulness Sands for seven miles to the mouth of the River Crouch. Once there was only one light buoy, the Sunken Buxey three miles out. The sailing vessel that starts at the outer end in the dark with a head wind and just keeps beating back and forth cannot end up anywhere but in the River Crouch. There is no need to sound all the time, for once you have got an idea of the length of each tack, start sounding again when you judge that you are nearing the other bank. If the creek up which you are beating has a fork this can be avoided by making timed short boards out from the opposite shore when you reach the area in which you expect the fork to be.

If a head wind makes entering a difficult or unknown creek safe and simple, a tail wind is the opposite. The boat will be travelling fast and unless you have been very careful indeed with your reckoning, once you find yourself in shallow water you won't know which way deep water lies and immediately have a fifty-fifty chance of running aground in seconds. Of course you could tack to leeward, sounding shallow water each side of the channel, but one never does. On Good Friday some years ago in a rising gale from the north-east two yachts from the Medway arrived off the entrance to the Whittaker Channel after dark, bound for Burnham. They were swept over Foulness Sands and one vessel broke up, fortunately without loss of life. A parachute flare sent up wasn't seen by anyone on shore, which should be a warning to those simple souls who carry a firework kit around with them, confident that a flare or two will quickly summon a number eleven bus along to take them home! It is always easy to be wise after the event but they had the simple alternative of passing through the well-lit Spitway and following the light buoys all the way to a safe overnight anchorage in the River Colne from where they could have blown down the Rays'n to Burnham next day on the rising tide in perfect safety. I cannot over emphasise the folly of entering difficult harbours to leeward when there is any weight in the wind or swell left over from a previous blow. For years it used to be said that lifeboats were never lost in the open sea, only on the bar entering or leaving harbour. With modern improvements in design we now lose lifeboats in open water but the basic premise remains: sailor beware the lee shore.

Let us leave the horror stories and get back to exploring a new creek in suitable conditions. Once you run aground on a falling tide at least you have plenty of time to study the area thoroughly. In fact there is much to be said for going aground deliberately to study the area at low water, but no one will ever believe you! The first thing to do is to get the anchor out. If there is no dinghy this will have to be done on foot over the mud or sand, which brings us to the interesting question of where we can and where we cannot walk. A bit of poking with the sounding pole will give us an idea of how firm it is. Walking on soft mud is something of an art, calling for confidence and a slightly skating action. Nowhere is it more true that he who hesitates is lost. While you keep going things are great but once you stop and press in one boot to extract the other, it becomes a strictly spectator sport. At least when carrying out an anchor you always have a rope or chain with which to haul yourself back to the boat. I always like to get the anchor out towards deep water so that I can get the boat afloat as soon as there is enough water to lift her. If there is a swell when the tide returns the boat might well bump for ten or twenty minutes until floated clear of the bottom. A good heave on the cable will start her on her way to deeper water the first time she lifts. Remember that the boat that grounds on an Essex weather shore in the morning (last of the night's offshore breeze from the north-west) could well refloat late in the afternoon on a lee shore (the onshore breeze is from the south-east).

I use traditional knee length wellington boots for mud work. They need to fit well so that they do not stay behind in the mud as you walk forward. One minor irritation, especially for knock-kneed sailors is that mud on the inner side of each boot will transfer from one boot to the other as you walk, rising higher each time and getting onto the inner side of your trouser legs above knee level. This means mud on board and in the cabin. The answer is to walk slightly 'Frankenstein' fashion, preventing the boots from touching. Whatever you do when working in mud, some will stick to your clothing. Do not try to rub if off wet for it will only stick harder. Leave it to dry when it will brush off cleanly. Once boots have been in the mud they are not welcome on board until cleaned, but this cannot be done without water. Don't leave them stuck in the mud alongside the boat for they will float off very quickly as the tide returns. Tie them to a cleat (see fig. 5). I use a piece of shock cord with hooks at each end. Once wellingtons came with holes punched in them at the back just below the lip, presumably to tie them together in pairs. Since the advent of packaging in hygienic boxes such holes are missing but the office punch will suffice.

With the lightest of onshore airs it is possible to let the boat look after herself as the tide returns. I must confess that this is in the grey area of things that I do not recommend but do at times. Some years ago bound down the Thames on the early morning tide in light airs I had only reached the Lower Hope by low water. With several days hard demanding sailing behind me in the upper reaches, I was in no mood to try my luck beating down the ten miles of Sea Reach against the flood tide. Instead I eased over to the wide mudflats towards the historic and aptly named Mucking Creek, one of the few in the whole area which I had not explored. The mud is over half a mile wide and very soft. No channel is discernible, although the rising tide showed a preference for the slight depression that exists in the direction of the creek. Instead of anchoring, once the sails were down and stowed (but ready), I lazed in the cockpit in warm sunshine and watched the line of gleaming white gulls feeding along the waters edge, retreat in the face of the young flood. Now and again *Shoal Waters* would free herself and go forward for a few yards, then touch the mud again and stop. It is a method as old as time and gives us the popular expression 'Touch and go'. The advantage of the method is that the boat stays just afloat and tends to find the best water. If I had anchored until there was four feet of water under the keel I would not have known where to steer for the best water in the mixture of mud and sea ahead. The difficulty is to distinguish one from the other, for wet mud and sand reflect the sky just as well as the water. On most charts the mud is yellow and the water blue but in practice it is very different. One of the most frustrating afternoons of my life was spent trying to work my way through the Wash towards Kings Lynn under a scorching sun with light winds. There was as much sand as water at low tide and I just couldn't sort out one from the other, until darkness closed in and I was able to identify the buoys by their lights.

Early in 1980 Joy and I went out to see the East Anglian Offshore Racing Association fleet come down the Wallet on a race from Burnham to West Mersea. The wind was a rising northeaster and I decided to beach on the Gunfleet Sand north of the Spitway just before low water to watch and to have a meal in comfort. We knew the direction of the bank but had almost given up hope of finding it when the waves suddenly got smaller and there was sand, miles of it, reaching to the horizon. A little later while walking away from the boat, I was amazed to see a couple of canoes coming towards me. They said that they had tried to find the Gunfleet Sands before but had not found then until today when they saw me walking about. Sitting so low in the water, it was even more difficult for them as they didn't have our advantage of beating back and forth across a wide area to find smooth water that must indicate the drying banks to windward.

There is no pleasanter way of getting to know a new drying harbour than to arrive outside before low water in time to beach and spend an hour exploring the entrance on foot. It helps a lot if it is sand and gravel, but even muddy harbours have a gut or rill with the last of the water draining away over a hard bottom. Two particular instances spring to mind: Brancaster in 1951 and Rye in 1977. The latter has extensive harbour training walls which compel the winding river to enter the sea by a well-defined channel instead of spreading over a wide, shallow, ever changing bar. It was just a case of wading through a throng of happy swimsuited holiday makers and noting marks on the stone work which, when covered, would indicate sufficient depth in the channel for me to enter safely. Brancaster was very different. A wild sunset and wind rising from the north-west; onshore! Not a living soul in sight. I got over the side and walked the boat into the lee of a drying shingle bank crowned by the wreck of a coaster which must have been used for target practice during the war. A fiery red sun glowed through holes in the shattered ironwork as, armed with water-boots, compass and a notebook, I tramped along the creek bed, splashing through shallow muddy pools and a few tiny streams hurrying to get into the sea before the flood tide drove them back again. The channel winds among a maze of sand and shingle banks for over a mile. At the junction of the channel to Burnham Overy I found an area of flat sand which seemed to be the place to anchor for the night once I could get there. Now it is one thing to see a place when the tide is out but difficult to visualise it at varying states of the returning tide. Obviously any withies, buoys or even moored yachts can help (in fact moored yachts are often a good guide to the deepest water), but in order to get your boat in an hour or two after low water it may be necessary to make some marks of your own. Driftwood can be stuck in the mud or shingle can be piled up into heaps at the side of the channel to indicate when there will be enough water in it for your boat. Take particular care with the bearings which identify the spot in which you wish to anchor if, as in this case, I planned to get into my bunk once the anchor went down and let the boat ground on her own as the tide left. After getting into Brancaster I did just that, looking out about two o'clock in the morning when woken by the lively motion of *Zephyr* to find a wide expanse of water with just the tops of the banks visible under a brilliant moon, and again about ten the next morning to find her aground on smooth sand in bright sunlight as the tide began to flood. Such is the very essence of small boat sailing.

If in doubt about the depth, remember that, as a general rule, a steep shore means deep water close in and a shallow bank means shallow water. In other words, the angle of the beach or bank probably continues under the water. Smelling deep water and shallows is an art which can only be acquired over the years. Watch the water astern. Shallow water will cause a steep wake rising behind the transom, possibly muddy water at that. This was even apparent on the sail training schooner *Malcolm Miller,* which draws sixteen feet, when we took the North Channel out of Southampton just after high water. They have a simple way to check the tide level rather than the long and complicated reduction to soundings we teach at evening classes. Just phone up the nearest tide station and ask them how much water they have on the gauge!

Navigator Brian Hallows who came from Norfolk's shallow havens drew my attention to the steep wake and with a wink said, 'We know what that means don't we?'

Spits, bars or isolated shallow patches can sometimes be spotted by watching the appearance of the water. A smooth patch with a popple downtide is a certain sign of shallow water. The shallow patch is under the smooth water, not under the popple. Lastly beware of following other vessels unless you are certain that they draw more water than you do. Several chaps on the east coast have gone on the putty following a certain green gaffer that doesn't *look* as though she is a centreboarder drawing ten or twelve inches. I do carry a hoist of international code flags (November, Uniform, One, Foxtrot) to indicate that my draft is one foot, but few boats seem to carry a code book. Some years ago, in light airs off the Denghie flats, we deterred a following craft by getting the children to go over the side and walk. If you do follow other craft don't cut the corners. A catamaran followed me down the curving edge of the Maplin sands one warm sunny afternoon. I was cutting well inside the buoys except for the Blacktail Spit where the sand dries high almost to the edge of the deep channel. He was clearly steering on me and catching up fast. I watched with keen interest when the yellow ridge of sand moved between us as my course became even more westerly. It was visible to me with the sun at my back but not to him facing the sun. He was in no danger and I thought of the classic remark of that grand old man of east coast yachting. Francis B Cooke, 'That there is something not altogether displeasing about the misfortunes of one's fellow men'. Suddenly the cat stopped getting any closer and then the sails fluttered down.

All in all, learning your area wherever it may be is a wonderful experience that can be relished over several years. Keep a log both for future pleasure and for recording times and courses sailed in varying conditions. Stick at it. The more you sail the more you learn; the more you learn the more sailing you will be able to get into your limited time. Suddenly the whole area will be your playground. I started exploring the Thames Estuary in 1949 and after a quiet period while my family was young, launched *Shoal Waters* in 1963 to tackle the business seriously. Each year I seemed to be able to do bigger and better trips until 1970 when things seemed to click. To use a modern expression, I got it all together. It took me eight years to cover the first ten thousand miles and just five to sail the next. I am still polishing up the finer details.

Chapter Six

Choosing an Anchorage or Overnight Mooring

'It's all right for you,' said one of my evening class members after a slide show of a particularly attractive area. 'You know where you can and cannot anchor. How can we tell?' This brought me up with a jolt. A generation is emerging today who are unable to cope with personal freedom. They are so bludgeoned with 'No Parking' signs, signs showing parking only on alternate Shrove Tuesdays when there isn't an 'R' in the month etc. that the conception that you may anchor where you see fit is almost beyond them. That this freedom has to be exercised with responsibility and concern for other people on the water is even more difficult to get over.

Of course in small crowded harbours you go wherever the harbour master allocates you a berth and the same applies in marinas. This simplifies the problem and there is a breed of sailor emerging who merely sails from one marina to the next I have even seen it suggested that some yachts would become uninhabitable if they didn't plug into mains electricity once every twenty-four hours. It is all very well for chaps like myself with a choice of hundreds of possible anchorages during a fortnight's holiday cruise, but quite different in other areas. Some years ago I cruised north to Bridlington, Scarborough and Whitby and realised just how lucky we are in the Thames area for they have no other choice but those three harbours over fifty miles of coast. One large sailing vessel bound for Scottish waters did lay outside Bridlington overnight rather than dry out in the harbour and was rammed by a fishing boat, presumably on autopilot while all the crew gutted fish I suppose that there is a feeling of security for the boat in a marina and with a large crew it is nice to get most of them out of the way most of the time that they are not feeding or sleeping. On the other hand marinas tend to be noisy places, the pontoons creak and groan and someone is bound to have left his halyards clanging away. Lastly and most important of all, they cost money. Charges for short stays have to be high for it is the regular customer who really pays for these expensive structures. Any berths reserved for visitors are probably occupied only one or two nights a week during the summer and charges must reflect this. To make matters worse for small boats, there is often a minimum charge and this can be based on a boat as long as thirty feet. Anyway, I tend to use a marina rather less than once a year.

Having said that you can anchor anywhere, there are some obvious restrictions. Don't anchor in shipping lanes to impede commercial vessels, but this is no problem as there will normally be plenty of water just inside the line of navigation buoys, provided you don't mind the wash of passing vessels all night. Anchoring over oyster beds is not allowed but I regularly anchor and dry on the mud at the side of them, it's good sense not to be anchored on the starting line when a race is about to start, and that just about covers the restrictions on where you can anchor.

Now for the question of where you want to anchor. Depth is a major consideration. Heaving up an anchor and chain (or wet rope which may have picked up fragments of sharp shell that cuts your hands) has a strictly limited entertainment value, so the shallower the water the better. Getting the anchor snagged round old moorings is a constant worry. One easy answer is to put your anchor where you can get at it at low tide, or at least reach it with a boat hook. Provided the boat does not ground, the shallower the water the better. Perhaps the most important consideration is shelter, for life inside a small boat in rough water, particularly with the wind against the tide so that she swings beam on to the waves every few minutes, is sheer hell. For a tantalisingly short moment she will ride head to wind and cease to roll. Then she will swing round beam onto the wind, dipping first one gunwale and then the other into the water. As she turns back head to wind the rolling slowly diminishes to be replaced by pitching. Then the whole sequence is repeated ad infinitum until the tide turns. Dry land to windward is the answer, but remember that the wind can change so I like to anchor just after a weather forecast. Remember that the tide will turn if you are staying overnight and that at spring tides high water occurs during the small hours in the Thames Estuary. It is possible to creep up Tollesbury Creek in the evening at low water and find a quiet spot to anchor with high banks all round but six hours later all the saltings around will be under a wide expanse of open water. Add a strong wind and you will have a rough hour or two until the tide falls a few feet.

The narrower the creek the better the shelter but there is a danger that the boat will swing over onto the shallows on either side and ground soon after high water while you are asleep. This means a lot of time wasted if you planned to sail off near the bottom of the tide, over and above any immediate discomfort for those on board. Even more disastrous, the boat could settle on a steep bank and topple right over as the tide falls. Don't anchor among moorings as you will almost certainly get hooked on one of them. Far better pick up one of the moorings but don't forget to have a look at the chain carefully. The links may be paper thin and have lain unused for years. There is always the chance that the owner will turn up at sunset, so don't leave the boat unattended without permission. In most anchorages there are some moorings that are not in current use. Evidence of this is the mooring line hanging from the top of the buoy. If it is slimy with weed you can bet your bottom boots that it hasn't been out of the water and onto the foredeck of a boat for months. Don't be put off by the 'Home Tonight' syndrome. The chap who put it on his buoy is probably laying on someone's mooring in the next river this night. For sound undisturbed sleep nothing beats drying out for the night. Of course it can only be done when high tide occurs morning and evening, neaps in my area.

'I suppose you just run her up the beach' was the opening remark by a deep water friend of mine. Nothing could be further from the truth. Choose carefully. The bottom must be level. If you plan to go ashore once the tide has gone it must be firm enough to walk on. Most important of all, it must be free of stakes, large stones and discarded Austin seven engines. The old bargeman's trick of arriving before the patch on which you plan to dry covers is the real answer, but often the small boat man only looks for a spot after the ebb has set in. Seaweed with bubbles in the leaves only grows on solid material, never on mud. If you see any, find out what it is growing on. I like to get over the side and walk about to make quite sure. The heading of the boat is important. It's best to lay head to wind as then you can sit in the cabin with the hatch open. Other considerations may be your wish to admire either the sunset or the sunrise. If there is any danger of vicious wash from passing craft that might burst right into the cockpit as the boat dries or refloats, point the boat towards deep water. I find it very satisfying on the Thames when drying out for the night to watch through the port as the frustrated wash from a passing tug hurls itself furiously on the mud between me and the river. An opening port is an asset here as one can reach out a hand and give the two finger sign!

Getting the boat level is very important, for if your bunk is high at the foot it can make sleep difficult to come by. Heeling one way or the other is easy to correct on smaller craft as a piece of driftwood can be put under the bilge runner on the lower side after the tide has left. Mooring the boat so that you can step straight ashore onto the saltings is ideal and I have often found a piece of driftwood to make a gangplank. The snag is that this means drying near high water. In this area each high water after 1500 hrs is lower than its predecessor until neap tides at 2100 hrs. I learnt this the hard way. After a rough handling in the Swale I crept right up into the saltings near Lower Halstow against the cherry orchards at 1600 hrs on a Wednesday. The tide came back for me the following Monday at 1100 hrs! To make matters worse, I was bound westward and the wind blew from the east while I was trapped and went westerly the day I floated. Make certain that the tide has dropped at least a foot before the boat grounds. Presumably the idea of laying against the saltings is to get ashore. Make certain that your chosen bit of grass is attached to the sea wall. Often large areas are cut off from the wall by guts and rills six feet deep or more. Check before you dry.

At springs with high water late in the night it is more difficult. With a westerly wind I often dry in Stansgate Creek soon after high water, against the western marshes with the boat level enough to live aboard and lay a plank to the saltings where I love to light great driftwood fires. Apart from the pleasure it gives me, wood that goes up in smoke will not go walkabout again at springs to become a danger to other craft. Once the tide has gone, I carry the anchor out towards the channel to its full scope of fifteen fathoms, so that when she floats in the small hours she swings out into the channel, either by wind or tide, and is afloat when I wake next morning ready to take the last of the ebb to the river mouth. A question that arises in such a case is the use of an anchor light. I always put one up but it could confuse other craft coming into the creek after dark while I am still high and dry. An incident outside the Crouch many years ago is still on my conscience. It was brilliant moonlight with wind from the west. We started down the River Blackwater as soon as the boat floated at dusk and arrived off the mouth of the Crouch about an hour after high water. There was no future in beating into the river over the ebb so I anchored just over the mud on the Northern edge of the channel, I didn't want to wake up to find the boat rolling with wind against the tide when the flood started as this is a sure recipe for seasickness and a headache. The boat would be afloat for several hours as low water was at 0500 hrs, so I put up the anchor light. Next morning she was aground on a little spit with cheerful waves advancing on each side as the sun rose clear out of the blue sea. By the time I had made a cup of tea and dressed, she was afloat and off we went up river. Aground just near us was a large keel boat laying over at a horrible angle. The crew stood huddled in the cockpit and never gave us any acknowledgement. I guessed that they had left Burnham at about 0200 hrs, half ebb, to round the Whittaker and take the flood into the Thames and had assumed that our light meant we were afloat in the channel.

The ability to dry out in comfort is never more valuable than when the forecast is horrible and you seek a 'Hurricane Hole'. In October 1980 the forecast was gale force winds from the west going round via south to north-east with rain galore. I found a flat area south of Skippers Island in Walton Backwaters, where a bend in the creek meant that there could never be a long scope of water to windward, whatever way the wind blew and lay there from 1400 hrs Friday to 1000 hrs on Saturday. When I ventured round into Walton Creek, which accepts the swell from the North Sea at high water, I found keel boats large and small having so rough a time that some of the people on board had skinned up and were sitting on deck, presumably because conditions below were so untenable.

Remember that drying out is a decisive step. Once the tide has gone you are there for some hours until the water returns, if you find that you do not like the neighbours there is not much you can do. They can vary from small boys throwing stones to a herd of cattle with a keen interest in boats (see fig. 6). On Saturdays watch out for people rigging loud speakers and/or unloading stacks of canned beer. Beach parties are becoming popular with the lager louts. It pays to have a good look round while waiting for the tide to leave.

Lastly, do not hesitate to anchor in the open when the sea is smooth. Have the sails ready for a quick get away, but there is little danger if you listen to all the forecasts. It was done a lot more years ago than it is today, but with an increasing tendency to charge for entering harbours and even rivers and creeks in some areas, I feel we shall see more of it in the future. One only has to look at the boats out rod fishing to see where one can anchor in safety, albeit uncomfortably. It is even possible to dry on an open beach but see that there is a ridge towards open water so that the boat floats in smooth water when the tide returns in case an onshore breeze springs up. In 1977 *Shoal Waters* was with the Fleet in the Solent for the Jubilee Review and I wanted an overnight mooring ready to join the fun next day. Bembridge seemed too far south if the wind failed next morning for the tide would be foul. I sailed in towards the shore east of Ryde about two hours before high water and was warned by two youngsters in a motor boat not to go any closer to the shore as there was a sandbank ahead of me. It was just what I wanted! I sailed over in eighteen inches and found three feet close to the shore. This anchorage served me well for two nights. The only difficulty was to know how much chain to put out. I used too much. With light wind and a lazy tide the boat swung to half the chain and thus settled on the sand within a few feet of the anchor. She could have landed right on it!

The architect of Britain's naval might in Edwardian times, Admiral Jackie Fisher was wont to boast, 'Englishmen may sleep safely in their beds,' presumably because of the protection provided in an increasingly hostile world by the long grey lines of ironclads for whose construction he had been largely responsible. I have a delightful photograph of *Shoal Waters* on the sand at Ryde in 1977 guarded by three carriers, many cruisers and a full supporting fleet, while I slept safely in my bunk.

Chapter Seven

What has the Weather in Store for You Today?

An American tourist visiting an English stately home, asked the head gardener the secret of such a superb lawn. He explained how the ground was prepared and the seed sown, then he added, 'Just mow it regularly for four hundred years.'

I am afraid that the sailor who wants to know what the weather will bring in this area today is up against the same problem. The chap who has been sailing for ten years will have a better idea than the one who has just started, and the chap with twenty years behind him will know that much more. Experience is the key. This is not much help to the newcomer. How does he start? Well of course there is no shortage of books on the subject and lectures aplenty. The snag is that they are all concerned with deep theory. I can understand the subject in the classroom, but cannot relate it to the conditions around me when afloat. I remain one of those sailors who think of a cold front as a topless waitress in an Eskimo cafe. Careful observation of weather experts afloat suggests that they do no better. Some years ago when speaking at a weekend sailing conference, I got there in time to hear the previous speaker on weather lore. He was an ex-wartime air force weather expert called in at short notice. His theory was completely different from the modern ideas. Although not a regular sailor he had sailed with the chap running the course and spoke of being becalmed off Clacton in mid-afternoon when there should have been a westerly wind force four. This puzzled him but the answer was simple. It was a hot summer day which brings in an onshore breeze up to force four or even five. This cancelled out the forecast wind, hence the calm.

I relegate books on weather forecasting to the same shelf as the home lawyer and do-it-yourself doctor; interesting to read but when you have to go to court or are sick, get a lawyer or a doctor. When you want to know the weather forecast go to the Met men. Unlike the chap who wants a solicitor or a doctor, there is no need to phone for an appointment. Just tune into the radio and get the latest expert opinion. Become a weather forecast addict, then add in known local variations and you are an your way. That it serves me well is shown by the fact that the engineless *Shoal Waters* has never failed to get home on Sunday evening or at the end of a holiday through lack of wind.

The main shipping forecasts on fifteen hundred and fifteen metres at 0045 hrs, 0555 hrs, 1355 hrs and 1750 hrs are the basis of the system. Local radio stations give increasingly useful advice (including the times of high water, in case your have forgotten your tide tables or have a son with a boat). There is a very detailed telephone weather forecasting service for local areas called 'Marine Call'. Details are available on handy, credit card sized cards from most chandlers. It is cheap enough when called from home but expensive when using a call box.

Before you try to interpret the main shipping forecasts study the areas they cover carefully. It took me years to realise the Thames area starts along the north Kent coast and goes right over as far as the Dutch coast. Most of our weather moves east and slightly north at about fifteen miles an hour so that what they forecast for the Thames is often already happening to the sailor at Burnham. In my experience the Dover area is generally more relevant to the Thames Estuary sailor south of Clacton. By listening to Thames, Dover, Wight, Portland and Plymouth one can get an idea of weather to come. If they are all the same and forecast reasonable winds you have got the sailorman's equivalent of the poker player's straight flush and should be able to come up with a winning trip. Remember that they have now changed the system so that instead of forecasting the average probable wind strengths they now give the strongest likely strength. The forecast is for the wind speed thirty feet above the water. Over the years you come to recognise the wind strength forecast in relation to your boat and the various areas in which you sail. If there are no gale warnings anywhere on the chart this is a comforting sign, but if your area is the only one without a gale warning then *watch it mate!*

The Met men tend to hang on to gale warnings long after the gale has passed, so do not let a gale warning deter you from making a short trip that can be completed in a few hours. Some years ago I sheltered at Upnor on the Medway in a north-west gale. At high tide at 1750 hrs the gale warning was still in force so I beached for the night instead of dropping lower down the river ready to take the morning ebb to Essex next day. On the news a few minutes later they announced that high-sided vehicles were being allowed over the Severn Bridge again. Next morning came in flat calm. It was half ebb before we got to the river mouth for a long slow haul over the flood to reach the mouth of the Blackwater at high tide to punch the ebb up river. I should have taken the hint about the Severn Bridge. In 1975, bound into the Thames for the Clipper Regatta, strong winds from the south-west forced me to give up in the Swin and cut across Foulness Sands to shelter in the Crouch. Throughout the long day I listened to every forecast, 1750 hrs brought me no comfort but I switched to Radio Medway to find that the wind would ease and set sail at once. Unfortunately I was setting out too late and met the first of the flood tide before getting round the Whittaker Beacon at the north-east corner of Foulness Sands. This lost me a couple of hours and once round the beacon, I had two hours less tide to help me into the Thames. At high water I ended up over the mudflats off the Isle of Sheppey. Fortunately by this time it was flat calm so I was able to anchor and sleep until the morning flood. Of course what I ought to have done was to leave the Crouch in time to round the Whittaker beacon at low water and listened to the forecast on route, ready to turn back if it was unfavourable. After all I had nothing else to do but sleep!

Numerous books explain the progress of the standard depression but the main thing to remember is that a blow from the south-west, tends to swing north-west and blow itself out. Rapidly improving visibility is the first sign of this.

The main weather pattern will be affected by the change from land to water and the dominating effect in the summer is the onshore/offshore breeze. As the sun heats up the area on a typical summer's day the land warms up quickly and air rises to give white fluffy clouds. The sea warms much more slowly and is relatively cool. Wind from the sea begins to move inshore to replace the air rising from the land. Obviously it will start earlier when the sky is clear from dawn, and later if cloud persists well into the late morning. This effect is first noticeable out in the estuary and gradually moves inshore. At sunset the breeze dies and the land cools rapidly, very rapidly indeed if the sky is clear, for cloud acts as a giant blanket keeping in the heat of the day. The sea remains the same temperature and is soon warmer than the land. It warms the air above it which rises and is replaced by air from the land. This gives us the offshore breeze overnight which can last well into the morning if dawn is cloudy. Between the two winds there will be a patch of calm weather which gives us a calm period at sunset and a much shorter one sometime in the forenoon. The latter can be very narrow, sometimes not much more than three of four hundred yards. Cruiser races out beyond the river mouth are very popular in my area when tides occur morning and evening. Several times I have been sailing north from the Crouch as a long line of racing boats leave the River Blackwater carrying spinnakers, while my glasses show that other craft well out to sea have already picked up the onshore breeze coming in from the south-east. One after the other the spinnakers collapse as they reach the calm patch and a few minutes later they are beating, still heading in the same direction. I remember running into the Blackwater around midday and meeting another craft running out. When we met he began to beat out of the river while we started to beat in.

As the afternoon progresses the onshore breeze moves steadily inland and I am told that it can reach Queen Mary reservoir near Heathrow airport by early evening on a very hot day. The only snag comes when you find yourself moving westward with the calm patch. At Easter 1978 I left Gravesend on the Thames just before low water at midday and went upstream with the spring flood. Sometimes the light wind was ahead, sometimes astern as the two systems battled it out over my head. After I anchored near the Woolwich Barrier at high water a steady south-east breeze blew until sunset.

Lucky is the sailor who takes his holiday when a high dominates the area with just a few isobars spread thinly over the weather chart, for offshore and onshore winds will be the rule. The onshore breeze can get up quite strong by late afternoon, sometimes force four or even five. The night breeze is a gentler fellow, more often force two or at the most three. While the onshore breeze can be gusty and turbulent the night breeze is delightfully steady. I believe that the explanation is that by day the air is warmest nearest to the ground and it gets cooler rapidly as one goes higher. At night the air is coolest nearest to the ground. Air consists of molecules buzzing round and colliding with others, to whom they impart some of their energy. By day the molecule knocked upwards will find itself in cooler air and continue rising. The one knocked downwards will find itself in warmer air and continue sinking. Thus turbulence increases during the day. At night the temperature gradient is reversed. The molecule knocked upwards finds itself in warmer air and falls back to its original level. The one knocked down finds itself in cooler air and floats up again. Thus as the night goes on the airflow becomes almost horizontal and a delight to sail by.

I remember leaving the River Ore late on Friday evening as the north-west offshore breeze arrived an hour after sunset. It was a gloriously clear night, just made for sailing. Hour after hour *Shoal Waters* chuckled along with a beam wind as the stars came up in the eastern sky and dived down in the west, while behind me the Great Bear pirouetted round the Pole Star. The sun rose clear out of the sea and killed the wind at 1000 hrs. The Buxey beacon was a few hundred yards away and as it was now high water I anchored for two hour's sleep. I woke at noon to find a good breeze coming in from the south-east which carried me into the Crouch as far as the mouth of the River Roach, and then brought me back to scrape through the Rays'n and take the next flood into the Blackwater. As the sun went down and the stars came out against the amber afterglow, I picked up my mooring after forty-eight hours and one hundred miles of memorable sailing.

One delightful feature of the Essex coast is that warning of an impending south-easterly breeze is given by tiny spiders who weave gossamer silk all over the rigging. One rarely sees the spiders themselves but in a flat, forenoon calm towards the end of the 1987 season while anchored opposite Bridgemarsh Island in the Crouch on water like a mirror, I watched a steady procession of minute spiders on long lengths of gossamer silk move slowly south across the river four to ten feet above the water. Those that missed my boat and rigging rose ten or twelve feet to clear the sea wall. The rest left the boat smothered like a ghost ship. Half an hour later there was a fine breeze from the south-east.

Things get complicated when a light wind is forecast. If it is easterly, it will supplement the onshore breeze to give a lively blow that will send yachtsmen reaching for the reef points muttering, 'I wish one of those b----y Met men was on the foredeck now! They never forecast this!' A light westerly will bring calm or a lighter onshore breeze. At night in easterly or northerly weather the offshore effect will cause the wind to back and this can be useful. *Shoal Waters* once jibbed at the thought of beating down the Thames into an easterly wind that would have given a rough old ride in Sea Reach by late afternoon. Instead we rested at Barking and took the evening ebb. By the time we got to Sea Reach I could point due east along the shore for a late night break at Hole Haven. Some years before, during a long spell of steady north-easterlies I left Hole Haven in the small hours and found a fair wind as far as the Blacktail Spit where we anchored to wait for the flood tide across the sands to Havengore. Long before we sailed on, the wind had followed the sun to go back north-east. In similar conditions on another occasion I sailed early from Southend over the flood and was able to point north-east to Havengore Creek. After passing under the old lifting bridge I anchored for breakfast in the lower River Roach. By the time I got underway again the wind had gone round north-east and I was able to steer due north through the Rays'n. Over the years one of the principal factors in the successful cruising of *Shoal Waters* has been the north-west winds that carry her down the river when high water occurs during the hours of darkness. Another factor that I experience regularly is calms, or at least lighter winds at sunrise and sunset.

Rain is largely irrelevant. Boats sail just as well as in dry conditions. No one has ever melted away in it yet! Winds tend to blow much harder later in the day and in periods of strong winds one can often snatch a passage in comfort by making an early start. Some years ago a boat from the Medway was lost on Foulness Sands late on Good Friday evening in north-easterly weather after a gale warning issued at 1400 hrs. That morning I left Heybridge soon after midnight and sailed to the East Swale, finding conditions so delightful that I went via the Edinburgh Channel to make the trip last longer. Another time I had to cancel plans to sail from Fambridge with the ebb at 1400 hrs because the easterly wind had increased so much since we crossed the estuary from the East Swale starting in the small hours.

An important aspect of weather is visibility which can vary day by day and even hour by hour. A fine summer's day can bring haze down to a couple of miles, especially in easterly weather. Often one cannot see Bradwell power station from the Bench Head buoy just outside the river. For some reason visibility often improves dramatically at sunset. Coming out of the East Swale late one afternoon bound for Essex and home, visibility was very poor and I pondered on the dangers of crossing the Thames shipping lanes. Off the Middle Sands I suddenly realised that things had changed and I could pick out buildings on Foulness Island near Havengore eight miles away.

By contrast, visibility on dull and even wet days is often very good and features four or five miles away stand out clearly. Exceptionally good visibility is sometimes a hint of a hard blow to come. The best visibility I can remember came soon after dawn north of the East Barrow Sand following a light shower. Looking south-east, I could pick out a strange cloud formation which didn't move, it fascinated me for it looked like two enormous lug sails. The glasses revealed the tops of power station cooling towers from which these clouds issued. It could only have been the power station at Richborough, twenty two miles away. As far as I can remember it didn't bring a blow.

Fog is the other side of the coin. It comes in two brands, land fog which goes with calms, particularly at dawn after clear nights in spring and autumn, and sea fog which can occur anytime including hot summer days. Far from being associated with calms, the latter usually arrives with a rising wind, sometimes up to force five or six. One summer afternoon I lay at Walton Stone resting, ready for a trip south with the night flood, when it suddenly went cool and I looked out to find the boat wrapped in cotton wool. Fog horns blared away to the north as steamers struggled in and out of the busy port of Harwich. Sailing in fog by daylight is one thing; sailing in fog at night is another, so I left at once for the Blackwater, sounding my way north along the edge of the Pye Sand until there was enough water to steer due east. Suddenly I shot out into bright sunshine where several bewildered yachts searched for the entrance somewhere in the white blanket that still obscured everything westward. The rest of the run home was as clear as a bell.

Sailing in fog is safe enough in shallow water away from the shipping lanes, especially if you have tan sails which can be seen fairly well. If your boat has white sails and a white hull it is for all practical purposes invisible. The sailorman has one advantage over the motorboat in fog for he can hear power vessels and even voices from other craft under sail. In a possible collision situation steer away from the noise of the other vessel as this will increase the time in which to take avoiding action once you can see each other. If you are making two knots and the other vessel is coming your way at five knots the distance between you is decreasing at seven knots. If you steer away from him it will be reduced to three knots. If you have faith in human nature you can of course hoist a radar reflector but sail as if it is not there. Staring into a radar screen is not much fun. Remember the vessel which rammed Southend Pier a few years ago!

An overcast night reveals the direction of lighthouses and light ships below the horizon as the light shines on the base of the clouds. The moon will be helpful even with ten tenths cloud and, of course, makes night sailing simple when the skies are clear. There is a regular pattern between the phase of the moon and the time of moon rise and set. The new moon appears in the western sky soon after sunset and soon follows the sun out of sight. By the first quarter the moon will appear high in the southern sky at dusk and set about midnight. The full moon will rise in the east in all her glory as the sun sets in the west, and last until dawn. After this, moon rise gets later each night and the yachtsman planning to sail into darkness cannot expect much help until the small hours. The dying moon will loom out of the eastern sky just ahead of the sun; pretty to watch, especially when accompanied by Venus, the morning star, but not much help to the chap making an early start. On an impulse one Easter after a trip counter clockwise round Canvey Island, the sheer exhilaration of the beat down Sea Reach with the spring ebb into a wind north of east, tempted me to pass the River Medway and press on round the Isle of Sheppey to the East Swale. I hadn't thought out the time of darkness, moon rise or the extensive flats far out from the island. Too late I realised that I would be running towards an unlit lee shore in the dark with no moon to help me, for it would not rise until after midnight. It is out of the question to sound round the edge of the sands as the Columbine Spit juts out to give a blind channel. As luck would have it I found the unlit Columbine buoy in the last glimmer of daylight thanks to my seven by fifty glasses, I thought of a remark made by a shop assistant that, 'These are really too good to take to sea.' The pleasant surprise of a light on Pollard Spit buoy helped me on my way and I was very thankful to anchor in the lee of the great whale of a sandbank that is the Horse Sand just before low water to get the stove going under some soup. By the time I was ready to go on with the young flood the moon was up there to guide me on my way to a mooring near Elmley Island.

Visibility affects the distance that light buoys can be picked up in the dark and haze seems to have a serious effect on green flashing starboard hand buoys which are never as visible as white ones in the best conditions. Red flashing buoys are better but not much, which, of course, is why port hand buoys flashed an even number of white flashes in the days when the safety of mariners was the primary purpose of light buoys and the theorists were kept at bay by common sense and the hard school of experience afloat.

The one weather riddle that continues to bewilder me is how to tell if that dark patch of storm clouds looming up will bring wind, rain, both or neither. Of course if you are not in hurry, get any kites such as spinnakers or topsails down or even take all sail down and drift or anchor until it has passed over. The real problem arises on a coastal passage when you must make every possible yard before the tide turns against you. More than once I have reefed down, skinned up, and sat there bobbing about with hardly enough wind to blow out a candle and not enough rain to fill an egg cup. On the other hand I have sat huddled over the tiller in blinding squalls of almost unbelievable ferocity wondering what would have happened if this lot had caught me with full sail set.

After a squall there is usually a quiet period before the wind settles down again and this can often be used to advantage, such as getting under way or crossing open water. In strong northerly winds we tore down the River Blackwater one August afternoon hugging the northern shore to find smoother water. While we wanted to get to Burnham I just didn't fancy crossing the wide open mouth of the river with this wind. As we passed Mill Creek and the site of Old Tollesbury Pier a vicious squall hit us and we were thankful for the slight shelter of the low marshland. Twenty minutes later it had passed over and in the following quiet spell we sailed over onto the now uncovering Denghie Flats, reaching the first two wreck beacons before the wind really piped up again. This put over a mile of shallow water to windward of us, which kept the steep waves mercifully small. The weight of the wind can be gauged by the fact that we left Heybridge lock at 1445 hrs, called at the Blackwater SC jetty for a moment and reached the Crouch Buoy eighteen miles away at 1815 hrs!

At the other extreme there are quiet almost windless days when occasional mild squalls bring welcome breeze to get the boat moving. Probably our most critical trip is from the Thames Estuary to Yarmouth to get onto the Norfolk Broads river system. Having no engine, we must go in with the flood tide. We dare not tackle the trip in strong onshore winds and cannot sail into the harbour over the strong ebb tide with an offshore wind. A few years back it looked as though our overnight passage was going to be wasted as the light airs of the forenoon were barely sufficient to get us over the last of the flood tide. Fortunately three gentle summer rain squalls brought us enough wind to reach the pier-heads at Yarmouth with a few minutes to spare. Never have I struggled into oilskins more readily, for the alternative would have been to anchor outside for six or seven hours until the next flood.

All in all, I do not grumble about our English weather. In fact I think that it is nearly perfect for small boat sailors.

It provides sailing aplenty for those who want it and a ready excuse for those boat owners who would rather stay in the marina.

Chapter Eight
Tricks of the Trade

'One goes east and one goes west on the very same wind that blows. It isn't the gales, it's the set of the sails which determines the way that she goes.' This age-old rhyme sums up the ability of the sailor to make the best out of whatever Mother Nature chooses to serve up. Over centuries of seafaring, man has come up with all sorts of skills and techniques. Many of them have been forgotten and then rediscovered. Some have a general application while others apply locally. The following are some of the tips that I have used and found to serve me well. They are not in any particular order.

Rule one is to work the tides. Why refuse a free lift just because it means starting earlier or later than the accepted office hours? Remember that it is not a choice of fair tide or no tide; if the tide is not with you it must be against you. Think of the escalators on the underground. Sometimes you have three choices, up, down and a stationary one. At sea there are only two to choose from. How many people walk up the down escalator? If the key to a certain trip is the full use of a fair tide somewhere along the route make certain that you allow plenty of time to get there by the time that it turns in your favour. Nothing is more frustrating than struggling against a tide that already has begun to run against you knowing that if only you had started out a little earlier and got round into the other channel before it turned, that same tide would be helping you on your way instead of hindering you. A chap at the club was telling me how unkind fate had been to him. The flood tide had been against him all the way from the River Medway to the Spitway where he had hoped to pick up a fair tide into the River Blackwater. By the time he got to the Spitway it was high water and the tide turned against him for the rest of the voyage. I just hadn't the heart to point out that if he had left the Medway six hours earlier or six hours later he would have had a fair tide all the way. In this case his misery was compounded because his mooring dries and he had a long wait for it to cover with the next flood. Yes sir. Work your tides!

Of course this will mean sailing during the hours of darkness, a frightening experience at first but one soon overcomes that and settles down to enjoy it as an important part of the sailing game. People used to well-lit streets just don't realise how well their eyes can adapt to darkness once they are given the chance. The mast, the halyards and the sails, are clearly visible, even when there is no moon. In over thirty years of sailing I can only think of two nights when mist and rain made it impossible to see the shapes of the waves. The secret is to cherish your night vision by avoiding all bright lights. Don't use a torch or deck lights to get under way. Keep the cabin lights low and shield them from the helmsman. Train your eyes to see in the dark. Don't stare, let the eyes sweep round the horizon as there seems to be some evidence that we see best just off centre. Don't use a spotlight. It is a menace to yourself and what is more important, other river users, who may be blinded by it. Do use a pair of seven by fifty binoculars, the best that you ran afford.

On summer nights with a high water during the hours of darkness a number of yachts leave drying moorings in Maldon and drop down to a popular anchorage east of Osea Island pier so that they are free to sail when they please next day instead of waiting for the afternoon tide. Some try to find their way down river with a spotlight and get in a right old panic. They kill their own night vision and that of any other sailor who happens to be near them. Here and there they will pick out a moored yacht or even a navigation buoy if they are lucky, but, of course, cannot see the trees and buildings ashore to get an idea of their position. Some seem to want to sail at night with headlamps blazing away like the ones that they have on their cars and try to use a spotlight for that purpose, but there are no white lines to guide them on the sea. One chap tried to follow me one night by keeping the spotlight fixed on my back, blinding me. He was very lucky that I resisted the temptation to go into the shallows and scrape him off!

Bright moonlight makes things seem easier but on calm moonlight nights with patches of mist it becomes very difficult to judge distance. Moonlight and spring tides go together in the Thames Estuary and I have seen many craft left high and dry on the saltings trying to use the night tide. If you pick the very top of high water springs to ground you can be stranded for ten or twelve days. Areas like the marshes on the southern shore of the River Medway and Walton Backwaters are bewildering at night once the saltings are covered leaving just a few stretches of sea wall exposed above the wide water.

Some boats have port and starboard lights but no stern light. This is the most important one, for you are likely to see and deal with a craft ahead but it is the one from astern that will creep up unobserved on a sleepy helmsman. It is essential that he sees you in plenty of time. A cycle headlamp will be better than nothing and I still have a home-made brass fitting on the transom to take one. They are cheap but could save your life. Regular spraying with WD40 inside and out will prevent rust. Don't use low-footed headsails that obstruct your vision forward at night.

One danger that you cannot combat is floating wood. Massive timbers from old jetties that have finally succumbed to wind and waves, together with new timber dropped from commercial vessels abound in the Thames and drift all over the estuary, especially after springs when much stranded timber goes walkabout until it finds another home for a few days over neaps. Try to avoid sailing hard and fast in the dark. In any case it is long established practice to snug down at night, taking in any kites you may have put up during the day. A public service can be performed by towing home large timbers and the wood comes in handy. With a fair wind a fifteen or twenty foot log tows easily. For the same reason wood burnt on the saltings will cause no danger to small boats and I always try to start the fire on a large piece that cannot be carried to the fire. Such a fire will also consume some of the rope that has drifted onto the saltings before it floats off again ready to tangle with any unsuspecting propeller that comes within range.

Reduction to soundings is great fun at evening classes but a little tedious afloat. I use the teapot method when finding my way through shallows with a rising tide in light weather. Sail as far as you can and anchor. Put the kettle on and while it boils study the water and dry mud ahead and take careful bearings. By the time I have made the tea and drunk it, the rise of tide will equal the draft of my boat and I can sail where I saw water when I anchored. Of course if your boat draws six feet you may as well put a leg of lamb in the oven!

Beating along narrow rivers can be a bewildering business.

Sometimes you can tack right close to the bank while at other times the boat will fail to come round and stops against the reeds. It all depends on the current. If it is fair, keep out in the channel well away from the bank. For a start you will get more help from the current, but if you get in close to the bank in slack water before tacking, as the bow eases out into the stream while the stern is still in slack water it will be forced back into the bank. With a foul current keep on as long as you can, if the water close to the bank is deep enough. There will be slack water close to the bank and good progress can be made. Don't tack until the boat almost stops. Put the helm over, grab a handful of reeds to spring her round and once the bow eases out, the current will push her round onto the next tack.

In spite of all I said before, there is one occasion when it pays to stem the tide, albeit the last of the ebb. The prevailing wind from the south-west gives a beat home up the Blackwater and any wind over force three will kick up a fair old lop by half flood, the logical time to start from the river mouth to arrive at high water. The first two or three miles are the worst. A small cruiser inevitably finds itself beating home in conditions during which the owner would never leave his mooring, *if he was already on it*. The answer is to start four and a half hours after high water. By this time most of the ebb has run out. All the mud flats are uncovered and only the water in the channels remains to trickle out to sea. The wind and tide have been in the same direction for over four hours which helps smooth the waves. Furthermore, the water will be at least ten or twelve feet lower between the banks than at high water and that much more sheltered. Now the small cruiser will find much smoother water, which more than compensates for having to beat over the tide for the first ninety minutes, and she gets home with a dry crew. A similar situation can be found in most areas.

Watch the water ahead for shallow patches if it is that sort of area. Sometimes you can spot surf breaking on shoals and alter course accordingly. In lighter weather with small waves and a good flow of tide, shallow patches appear as smooth water with a popple downtide where water forced up by the shoal dives into deep water again. Watch for any change in the wave pattern. It may often be a trick of the light, a shoal or even a major piece of flotsam. Some years ago we went up the Thames and encountered several lumps of white floating stone, six inches thick and several feet long. It floated just level with the surface. Smaller weather beaten pieces of it can still be picked up on the saltings throughout the area. In fact as I write, a large block of it is supporting the front of my boat trailer in our workshop. In the late fifties we found several dead horses off the Buxey sand so be prepared for anything. One summer's night we hit something like a sand bank off Bradwell. It didn't touch the plate or the rudder, merely the bow which rose up for a split second or so. No damage was done. Was it a sleeping porpoise or seal?

Getting under way from a crowded anchorage, a marina or lock single-handed can be a problem with the wind aft so that you cannot hoist the mainsail before letting go, and the headsail is not enough. With a gaff vessel take the halyards aft and hoist some or most, of the sail from the cockpit in order to get clear before hoisting the sail property. It won't work with Bermudian rig as the slides will jamb on the mast. The reverse system can be used when entering a difficult place, for the gaff mainsail will fall down under the weight of the gaff as you ease the halyards.

A traditional Broads trick left over from the days before auxiliary power, to move a boat a short distance with a fair wind when the cockpit tent prevents the use of the mainsail, without disturbing the domestic arrangements, is to sail under jib and tent. At Whitsun 1979 I anchored late on Friday night near the tail of Canvey Island in Benfleet Creek, after a long day in the estuary from Heybridge out as far as the Margate Hook beacon. Saturday came in with a rising wind from the south-east and heavy rain hour after hour. We do not often get rain from the south-east in this area but when we do there is usually plenty of it. As the rising tide drove the last of the bait diggers off the protecting mud flats, *Shoal Waters* began to roll and pitch like mad. It was no place to stop. I got the anchor, unrolled the jib and blew a couple of miles up the creek to sleep the rest of the day away in comfort. By contrast Sunday came in perfect with wind from the south and I took the early ebb tide home via the Barrow Deep to arrive at the club by early afternoon on Sunday and flee home to dodge another awful day on Monday.

One of the principle uses of the tiny storm staysail is when beating into heavy seas. There is always the danger that however carefully one looks for a smooth patch in which to tack, a sudden steep wave will stop the vessel dead when head to wind and she will fall back on the same tack. If this happens two or three times the boat can well be aground in desperate conditions. I leave the headsail sheeted so that as the boat passes through the eye of the wind it goes aback and helps knock the head round on to the new tack. Watch the water alongside. The moment the boat stops and begins to gather sternway reverse the tiller, for once the boat goes backwards the rudder operates the opposite way. Of course this is out of the question with a large headsail and is one very good reason for having a very small one on *all* boats whatever the man at the Boat Show may say about the boat that he is trying to sell you with just one mainsail and one headsail being 'ready for sea'.

A sailing boat can be pivoted round weathercock fashion by use of the mainsail and headsail, a useful manoeuvre in tight waters. The effect can be even more dramatic in shallow waters where the bottom is soft mud if the centreboard is lowered and she pirouettes round it. This is particularly effective on the Norfolk Broads where in many places out of the main rivers there is no bottom as such. The water just gets thicker as you go down! On the same principle, the plate can be used as a brake to avoid ramming the bank, or over running the mooring when picking it up with just enough water to float the boat.

Another trick which I dare not recommend but which I do shamelessly in calm conditions is to use the plate as an audible echo sounder and instant draft reducer. Many a calmish Friday evening I have sailed out of the Blackwater until I could see the red flash of the north-west Knoll buoy and then turned south to pick up the white flash of the Sunken Buxey buoy outside the River Crouch. A glance at the chart shows that this puts me well over on the tail of the Buxey Sand. I have the plate down about two and a half feet so that it warns me well before the rudder touches. Then I settle back at the helm until the plate whispers, whereupon I pull it up a few inches and alter course west and then south-west to feel my way round the tail of the sand and the best water into the River Crouch. It gets shallower each year and these days it often means drying out and sleeping until the tide returns to take me into the river. Of course I do not do this if there is any suggestion of a swell which could strain the case, cause leaks or even bend the plate so that it couldn't be raised.

Picking up a mooring buoy becomes more difficult as one gets older and less agile. Towards the end of my fading forties I bought one of these grabbit boat-hooks ready for my feeble fifties. The hook is fitted with a sort of dog clip which keeps it on the buoy once it has been hooked. The whole fitting comes off the pole leaving a line from the hook leading through the bow fairlead to Samson post securing the boat. With a small boat no pole is needed as the hook can be attached by the helmsman. Just sail to bring the buoy alongside, reach out, clip on and get the sails down. As with everything else in this game, things can go wrong. I tried my new toy out in an east coast river with a line of buoys down the middle, one of which I decided to pick up while I had lunch. (Never anchor among moorings as you stand a fair chance of hooking some mooring chain). The headsail was furled, the plate pulled up and I tried to hook the buoy as it swept past in the strong tide but missed and unfurled the jib, dropped the plate and had a go at the next one. This time I forgot to lift the plate as I hooked the buoy and the boat swung round the wrong way so that the line from the bow passed under the hull *behind* the plate so that I was unable to hoist it. *Shoal Waters* was left struggling helplessly moored by the centre of the keel. The harbour master came out in his little clinker motor boat and tried to push the head round so that the rope would pass out under the stern to leave the boat swinging from the bow. The keel of his boat was not fitted with a projection to prevent a rope getting jammed between the transom and the rudder and this soon became apparent, leaving the two boats swinging helplessly in the swirling tide locked in an embrace that was positively indecent. Thank heaven no photographer was present. We got it all sorted out eventually but my mind always goes back to that moment when I am being introduced in glowing terms before giving a 'How To' lecture on some aspect of sailing. It serves as a reminder that however much you sail, you can still get in a muddle. I am tempted to say that the more expert you become, the more intricate the muddles in which you can find yourself.

Time and time again on the east coast a small boat will be driven out of one drying harbour at high water, make a fine passage to the next river with a westerly wind and then be unable to beat into that river over the ebb tide. One instance is the boat leaving the River Crouch for the Blackwater which must start at high tide to make certain of getting over the drying sands at the bottom of the Rays'n. Another is the boat that passes under the lifting bridge at Havengore, navigable only near high water, bound for the Medway with wind from the south-west and unable to beat in over the ebb tide. In each case the answer is to anchor and wait for the tide to turn. An anchorage out in deep water will be far too lively for comfort. Far better to anchor close in shore in smooth sheltered water and lift the anchor every hour or so as the tide falls to let the boat blow out into deeper water. The boat bound for the Blackwater can shelter under the lee of Sales Point and the boat for the Medway in the lee of the Isle of Sheppey. It is even possible to put a crew member ashore for shopping at Sheppey. Apart from the improved comfort, endless pleasure will be gained watching the banks uncover and the wading birds advance as the tide retreats. The centreboarder can let the plate down about six inches to warn of any danger of grounding.

Where flat sand and mud is miles rather than yards wide a similar trick can be tried on a weather shore. Faced with the prospect of getting back to the Crouch from the Thames in strong north-easterly weather and with no stomach for the beat round the Whittaker, I have taken the ebb out past the Blacktail Spit and then run in as far as possible over the ebb into one of the many guts that run into the sands. The water here is smooth enough until the tide rises to cover the sand to windward. When it gets too lively I lower the plate six inches, get the anchor, unfurl the staysail and run in until the plate touches, when it is whipped up smartly and the anchor goes down again, now in smooth water for half an hour or so. It is a long business but I know of less pleasant ways of spending a day. Of course this is only possible in a very shoal draft boat, probably eighteen inches or less.

Never make the inner end of the anchor cable fast to the boat with a shackle. Just turn it round the Samson post or some other sound fitting inside the forepeak and tie it with cord that can be cut in an emergency. In the sort of conditions that one is likely to want to slip your anchor because it is physically impossible to get it up, life below up forward will be hell and no place to battle with a rusted shackle. A club member had to leave his boat at Burnham some years ago after his first and only trip from the Blackwater. They had had such a rough time beating in over the ebb that his crew gave up sailing as soon as he set foot on shore. He left it anchored off the caravan site for the week and the club sailing secretary phoned me to help him out. As he would obviously leave at high water to take the ebb out of the river it could have been anchored well up on the wide mud flats where the anchor could have been stamped into the mud to make certain it would not drag, instead, he had anchored in deep water. It was flat calm on Friday evening when we joined the boat and found the anchor stuck fast. His principle problem was to get the boat back on her moorings at Heybridge and he agreed to buoy the anchor and slip it to be recovered later, (He had a caravan on the site). The cable was shackled to the inside of the stem. It was rusted solid and two of us spent a long time jammed in the tiny bow of the *Vivacity* with pliers, hacksaw and other gear to cut it free, easy in a flat calm but impossible in rough weather when sea sickness would have smitten both of us in minutes.

Of course do make certain that the inner end of the cable is fast in case the lot runs cut. Three turns and tie the end to the chain leading to the deck should do. One of my evening class members set off up the Thames in an Eventide and decided to anchor opposite Greenwich. He just hadn't realised how fast the flood tide was going and was unable to stop the chain running out. Two shackles (thirty fathoms) ended up laid along the bottom and he had no anchor, but at least the motor was running. Those patron saints of Thames yachtsmen the river police came along and hooked it up for him.

Buy your halyards and sheets at least a yard too long. This will enable you to at least treble their life by cutting off a foot every two or three years so that the wear caused by the block or cleat comes in a new place on the rope. So many yachtsmen end up with a perfect piece of rope except for just one bad patch and the whole thing has to be replaced.

Go over every detail of the boat regularly for weak points caused either by wear or bad design. When I first rigged *Shoal Waters* I had two fine shrouds each side fixed to a ring on a galvanised mast band at the hounds by one shackle. If that shackle had failed two shrouds would have been no safer than one. It took me nearly a season to realise this. Now each shroud has an eye spiced in big enough to go right over the masthead. If one fails it will not automatically affect the other.

Remember my six rules of successful cruising:

1. Never miss a fair wind and a fair tide. Such conditions don't come often. Make the most of them.

2. Never miss a chance to brew up. You may not need a drink immediately but it may be a long time before the next chance.

3. Keep dry as long as possible; better still stay dry.

4. Watch fatigue. As you get tired, cold and hungry and possibly a little scared, check and recheck your judgements and decisions. Be especially careful when you cease to be tired and feel you could just sail on for ever.

5. If at first you don't succeed *give up*. There will always be another chance to complete the voyage you have set your heart on. Leave the 'bash on regardless' stuff to the ocean racing boys. They have the boats and the crews to do it. You haven't.

6. Please, please don't scream for help unless you are in real danger. The chap who calls out the rescue services when his burgee halyard breaks drives one more nail in the coffin of our freedom to sail as and when we please. It's very precious in these bureaucratic times. If you cannot stand the heat keep out of the kitchen. If you cannot stand the trials and tribulations on the high seas please take up croquet.

With a little common sense and determination on your part that little ship can enrich your life immeasurably. It's worth a bit of effort to get it right.

Chapter Nine
Creature Comforts

One story of my early sailing days when I cruised in a leaky half-decker never fails to bring a roar of laughter from the audience. I fitted the sixteen foot *Zephyr* with a pipe cot thrown out by the new owner of a wartime motor torpedo boat. Tapered at one end, it fitted starboard side of the mast forward of the centre thwart and reached under the foredeck. This was before the days of cheap sleeping bags and I used ex-army blankets. There was room but only just and no prospect of my reaching down to my ankles. I kept a small cane handy with which I was able to push my pyjama legs down to my ankles once I had wriggled down into the bunk. Laugh they may, but such attention to details of personal comfort is the very essence of contented small boat cruising. It isn't the gales and storms or even the frustrations of fickle winds and foul tides, but minor matters such as a sock that goes walkabout as you dress for a two o'clock start on a wet morning that makes people resolve to give up sailing.

Keeping dry is rule two. Experience as a father has taught me that if a baby cries, the odds are that he has a wet nappy. It's an attitude that doesn't change much with the years. We are lucky today to have such a wide selection of water proof clothing to choose from. Buy the best and look after them well. Don't leave them encrusted with salt and crushed into a locker on Sunday evening when you leave the boat. Wash them regularly to remove salt and leave them spread out in a well ventilated place. Choice is a personal matter but it is as well to understand the basic types. They come in light, single material suits and those with linings for warmth and further protection. I prefer the former as they dry so quickly once the rain has passed over. In a long wet spell they can even be dried under the cockpit tent in front of the Gaz radiant heater, although I suspect that this can shorten their useful life if done too often. The material used consists of two essentials, the cloth which gives strength and the rubber or plastic which keeps out the rain (and keeps in condensation). This waterproofing can be inside or outside the cloth. My experience is that those with the waterproofing inside get unpleasantly clammy or even wet inside while those with the waterproofing outside are much more comfortable to wear.

I use separate jacket and trousers rather than the warmer and more waterproof complete suit, as so often the cruising man only needs the trousers when setting off in the early morning with the seats and coamings wet with dew but no spray about. Lastly and most important of all, wear waterproofs as little as possible. Constant wear reduces the proofing and the longer you wear them, the greater the condensation inside. It is particularly important not to wear them during the exertions of getting under way, unless it is bucketing down, as you will work up a rare old sweat that will make you uncomfortable for hours. Ordinary well ventilated clothing is so much more pleasant, especially if it is natural fibre. It never ceases to amaze me how much time some yachtsmen spend wrapped up like oven-ready turkeys when there is not a chance in a hundred of a drop of spray.

Even when alone, I like to get under way before skinning up and to chuck them off before bringing up. Even the lightest and best cut 'skins' are cumbersome to at least some degree and inhibit free movement so essential on a small boat. Leaving them in the cockpit whenever possible is a simple safety measure.

I must confess that I usually leave skinning up just one minute too late, i.e. after the first dollop of spray comes over, but here again we have a world of difference between jacket and trousers. If you get your seat wet it just won't dry unless you spend the rest of the day standing up with your back to the wind. On the other hand, one splatter of spray above the belt will soon dry. Lastly of course, there is the use of oilskins as a windbreak. I find it better to wear thick, close-woven garments of the duffel jacket type but there are limits and a jacket which is sufficient in force four from the south-west in June may let in far too much ventilation from a strong north-easterly in early March.

Inevitably your hands will get wet when handling wet ropes but do not let them stay that way for wet hands soon become sore hands. Dry them each time they get wet, either on newspaper or one of the modern synthetic window cloths. Incidentally, newspaper dries much better once it gets slightly damp. The back of the hand on the tiller must get wet in rain but it should be possible to keep the palm dry. Regular use of Neutrogena cream will prevent both soreness and cracking. Carry nail clippers and use them regularly, for a torn nail can be agony for days even causing loss of sleep with the danger that can bring. Hands have a busy time afloat and are worth taking care of.

Warmth is the next problem. Careful attention to the paragraph on staying dry will take you halfway there. I find natural fibres best, particularly wool. It is not just a question of garments that keep you warm once you have got them on. Sooner or later you are going to have to get dressed in the dark, on a cold spring morning to the rattle of rain on the deck above you in order to catch a fair tide. At such times even the keenest sailor asks himself, 'Is it worth it?' Whether he reaches out for a warm Vyella shirt or a nylon one can make all the difference to the answer. It's much the same with a warm duffel jacket that brings back childhood memories of snuggling up to your teddy bear, compared with the modern, chilly to touch, polyester jackets. In the very coldest weather I use a polar suit with nylon simulated fur on the inside. It is warm once you have had it on for a few minutes but I made the mistake of buying the top with a nylon zipper down the front. It is much easier to put on than struggling to get it over my head in a tiny cabin but oh, my! is that zipper cold in the sort of weather when I want to wear a polar suit?

Gloves are useful at almost any time of the year but cannot be worn in rain, for once wet they keep the hand damper than it would be without the glove. Remember to take them off each time you tack or adjust wet sheets. It may seem a nuisance but wet gloves are worse than useless and the activity of removing them and putting them back on after drying your hands all helps to keep those hands and fingers warm.

The cold that is most demoralising is the cold that comes up though your seat. A waterproof cushion is the answer here but how many boats carry them? When ever I buy a new car and the salesman asks if I want wood or upholstered seats I always go for the latter as experience shows that they are more comfortable. It is just the same with the boat. Even in wet weather a cushion still acts as an insulator. I recall sailing many years ago on an offshore racer where they used a small inflated inner tube for the helmsman's seat which proved popular. Lastly, remember to have socks big enough to tuck your trousers in. I suppose one could use bicycle clips, but...!

Before I deal with the refinements in the cabin, let us examine one process that does require a great deal of thought and discipline: that glorious moment at the end of a wet trip when the boat is moored, the sails are stowed (don't forget to frap the halyards), and the crew move into the warmth of a dry cabin. One reads of boats soaked from end to end and even crew members getting into their bunks in oilskins, but not in my type of sailing. On *Shoal Waters* wet gear stays outside. It's one thing to be wet, cold and tired on the helm, knowing that a warm dry cabin is just a few feet in front of you ready to be enjoyed once the anchor goes down. It must be another thing altogether to sit wet, cold and tired at the helm knowing that even at the end of the trip you face a wet cabin. The boom tent plays a key role here (see fig. 7). Ideally it should hang under the boom for with the tent over the boom, the wet sail will drip water for hours, but that is one refinement that I have not made yet. Once the tent is up, I try to dry off the seats a little, lay newspaper on the bridge deck and watching carefully for drips from the boom, take off my jacket and hang it up to dry or at least where it will not get any wetter. Then I slip out of my oilskin trousers leaving them still round my water-boots which remain standing up in the cockpit, fold the dry top to protect the boots and swivel into the cabin where dry carpet greets my stockinged feet. The 'carpet' is simply out of date samples often sold off in carpet shops for a few pence. A handy lighter sets the stove going and the Gaz radiant heater. The kettle goes on and as the temperature soars (one advantage of a small boat), I get down to shirtsleeves, search with a wad of kitchen roll for any drips that may have got in through the fore-hatch or the opening ports and then settle down to relax as content and luxuriously as only the sailing man can. The mountaineer, the explorer and even the weekend backpacker can get just as tired but they have to limit their gear to what they can carry on their backs. The sailor has no such restrictions. Even the smallest cruiser carries luxuries beyond their wildest dreams; a fine selection of tinned and dried food together with ample water for endless hot or cold drinks from stocks of tea, coffee, cocoa, Horlicks, Oxo, soups, cordial or pure fruit juice backed up with the remnants of whatever took my fancy on my last shopping trip in the way of bread, cakes, fresh or cold meat and fresh fruit.

There is of course a radio together with spare batteries and a supply of books. Don't throw batteries away the first time that they die on you. Store then for a day or so by which time they will have revived enough to give several hours more use; this can be repeated several times until they fade after ten or twenty minutes. The main use of the radio is for getting weather forecasts and it is switched on by pushing down a button, as distinct from turning a dial which is also the volume switch. This is important for getting that vital forecast when underway single-handed in conditions that prevent the radio being taken out into the cockpit. I can reach into the cabin to switch on with the other hand on the tiller. Over and above this, many people in this television age forget the wide variety of entertainment available on radio from serious talks to music and comedy. Don't panic the first time you switch on Radio Four in the small hours and find your watch has gained an hour. It will be the world service and all time checks are in

Greenwich Mean Time. I tumbled out of my bunk and dressed in a panic the first time I tuned in!

Four gallons of drinking water is carried in one-gallon cans. One four gallon can is much cheaper to buy than four one gallon ones, but the smaller cans are so much easier to handle, whether lugging them from some remote tap or merely reaching out of the sleeping bag having forgotten to fill the kettle for the morning tea before turning in.

Once you have eaten and see no immediate prospects of sailing on, what better way of spending the time than catching up on sleep? The cushions are four inch Dunlopillo. We each have two sleeping bags, both essential in the cold weather at the beginning of the season and often used during cold spells in summer. Over the years I have worked out a routine to make the most of these opportunities, for remember that fatigue is one of the major limiting factors in your sailing. Boats never tire but crews do. It is just not enough to be able to complete the planned trip, you must have something in hand in case things go wrong. Recent sleep is like money in the bank. For breaks of up to two hours I stretch out on the bunk with my feet aft and an unzipped sleeping bag over me. This way I face aft and can see out of the hatch which is rarely closed. For breaks of two to four hours I get into the sleeping bag properly, but merely slip off my sailing trousers and put on pyjama bottoms. For anything over four hours I bed down properly. After all, four hours below is the standard watch break of seafarers over the centuries. Don't scorn the hot water bottle. In fact early and late in the season we never let the sleeping bags cool down, reheating the water over breakfast and during the day. If the cold has got into your bones and you get into a cold bag it will take an hour or two for you to warm through and drop off the sleep. Slip into warm pyjamas, a warm sleeping bag with warm soft pillow and sleep comes within minutes.

Over the years I seem to have got a reputation for sailing day and night and doing without sleep. Nothing could be further from the truth. The secret is that I am prepared to sleep as and when the tide dictates. Any inconvenience to routine is more than made up for by the experience of sailing under the moon and stars and through endlessly variable sunrises and sunsets. I love most aspects of sailing but among the most precious memories are those when I have laid snug and warm in some safe hurricane hole and listened to the elements doing their worst outside the confines of my tiny life-support capsule.

While it is important to be able to deal with bad weather when it comes, don't let us become obsessed with it. Most of the time it is fine with useful working breezes. Over twenty-five years cruising I cannot recall a season with more than two days when it rained most of the day. Even 1980 only produced one really wet day among the seventy or eighty I spent on board. The delightful facts are that most days are dry and the sun shines at least half of the time. Then meals can be prepared with the boat head to wind, the hatch wide open to give an endlessly changing panorama of sky, clouds, sea birds, the waves of the receding or advancing tide and boats of all types. Better still, we can eat out in the cockpit and then sit with our backs to the cabin and doze away the time. At times the sheer heat becomes unbearable and drives us into the cabin to stretch out on the bunks with the fore-hatch open to give a cool breeze.

Comfort underway for the helmsman is essentially built in with the design of the seats and coamings. Some years ago I helped a friend take a well-known brand of small cruiser from the Blackwater to the Norfolk Broads. By the time we got into Lowestoft I had become convinced that the chap who laid out the cockpit must have served an apprenticeship with a firm of torture chamber fitters. There was just no way that one could sit comfortably at the helm. The only answer to such a boat is to sell it and look more carefully when you buy the next one. Certainly the cockpit on *Shoal Waters* is comfortable. I can sit facing forward with my back against the after bulkhead and the tiller under my arm, on the weather side with my feet braced against the lee comings or sit to leeward in light airs. A recent addition has been rope grommets made fast to the after-side of the cabin top on each side that can be held in heavy weather by the helmsman. My wife and I use these much of the time.

All the sheets and centreboard hoist are to hand. Extra clothing such as sweaters, gloves, cap, sunhat or sou'wester are to hand inside the cabin and the makings for various drinks are handy (see fig. 8). Most important of all, I can see over the cabin top and under the sails to carry out the requirements of the international rules to keep a good lookout, not to mention the safety of the boat and crew. Sitting there at the helm watching the sea miles slipping away under the stern is my idea of heaven, just sheer heaven. So comfortable is the cockpit on *Shoal Waters* that I never miss the chance in fine weather to sit there with the tiller under my arm on the mooring at Heybridge whilst the last of the tide runs out before walking ashore.

Chapter Ten

No Dinghy

Perhaps the biggest problem for the small boat sailor is the dinghy with which he can get to and from the shore when the boat is on a mooring or at anchor. It is possible to build a little cockleshell which tows well and will carry two people ashore provided that neither of them sneezes on route. Such a craft will prove useless to get to and from your mooring with a load of gear. At times you will want to get to and from your mooring in bad conditions. A sturdy dinghy is essential for this but it will be too heavy to tow behind a small cruiser and should be left on the mooring ready for when you return. There are of course inflatables but what do you do with all that wet rubber or plastic when deflated? Folding or collapsible dinghies have been around for at least a hundred years but the problem remains of stowing all that wet wood and canvas on board. With a keel boat there has to be a dinghy but for the shoal draft cruiser, particularly the centreboard craft, it is possible to cruise without a dinghy at all. Personally I can never understand the mad rush to get ashore, even at weekends. I know it is the traditional 'jack tar' attitude but this came from voyages of months or even years. I believe that most of Nelson's seamen had been afloat for over two years by the time the battle of Trafalgar was fought.

Let's face it, I shan't get afloat today, I didn't get afloat yesterday and shan't be afloat tomorrow. The same can, I am afraid, be said most days of the year. Once I am afloat I often stay on board from Friday evening until Sunday evening. Careful scientific tests have shown that forty-eight hours isolated on board a small boat have never proved fatal yet.

If we accept that no small boat can perform well and tow a dinghy, how do we get ashore? Firstly there are marinas and often there is no charge for brief stops. A number of places have public jetties where a boat can be left for short periods. Some get very crowded and a boat left unattended might well be damaged by other craft coming alongside, particularly working craft. With a crew, one member can go ashore shopping whilst the other anchors the boat a few yards from the jetty and returns to pick up when hailed. Years ago it was possible to anchor near rowing ferries and get the ferryman to put you ashore but in most places these days 'No one pays the ferryman' because there isn't one.

The best plan for the small boat is to beach and walk ashore. This will call for a pair of Wellington boots. If the shops are far away the boots can be hidden in the grass near the sea wall when you change into shoes. The tide is the vital factor here. Perhaps the simplest way is to dry an hour before low water which will give you two hours ashore before the boat refloats, although I like to get back soon after the tide turns as it can come swirling back very quickly. Be particularly careful if the boat is left as far out as at Southend, for the tide runs in over the mud and sand very strongly. If possible find a hard or some place where a firm beach is adjacent to water at all states of the tides. Such places are necessary when going ashore for a quick shopping trip on a rising tide. Get out all the anchor chain and carry the anchor as far up the beach as possible. If you still think that it will be covered on your return, tie some line to the crown and carry this inshore as far as it will go and fasten to a stick or large stone or better still, a Broads style rond anchor. On your return you can pull on this and get the anchor and thence the boat. This system has the advantage that the boat will be afloat instead of scraping back and forth on the beach, possibly with damage from the wash of passing craft. It has the further advantage that passers by are not likely to tamper with the boat, an increasing worry these days. Towards the top of the tide it is often possible to find three or even four feet of water next to the saltings and step ashore onto the grass. One trick here worth trying is to get out enough chain to anchor the boat and make fast, flake down the chain on the foredeck and then place the anchor, crown outboard, on the foredeck with a line to the crown. Push the boat out holding the line. When it is far enough out, jerk the line, the anchor falls into the water taking the chain with it and you have the boat moored safely off the bank with a lazy painter at the bank with which you can retrieve it when needed. In my first epic voyage in 1949 I did this, at Snape, at the head of the River Aide and walked half a mile to the village to get stores and a paper. There were no papers but the shopkeeper said that he would have one if I came back in half an hour. There was no paper when I returned, just a village policeman waiting to catch one of the two chaps who had absconded from the local borstal at Hollesely Bay the previous day. I told him that I had sailed there and we walked to the bridge to see the boat riding proudly in midstream.

'Where is your dinghy?' he asked. I showed him the lazy painter in the grass and this convinced him after which we yarned on the lovely old bridge until the ebb started and it was time to leave.

Walking ashore from the boat as the tide rises when you plan to return before it dries again is tricky. You may work out your tide times but the danger is that the boat will drift or blow towards the shore and dry soon after high water before you return. If you do not leave enough scope of chain to combat this, she may drag anyway. My trick, in these circumstances, is to anchor the boat after running up the beach or mud with all gear ready to go ashore. Then I get out more than enough cable for any possible rise of tide and trample it into the mud by the bow of the boat. As the tide rises the boat will take up the cable but no more than is needed for the rise of tide. This reduces the swinging area to a minimum, and increases the chances that she will still be afloat on your return. Of course you will have some very muddy chain!

There are endless possible permutations of wind and tide to contend with but there are answers to most of them. Perhaps the most difficult is with an onshore wind on an open beach. I adjusted the cable so that she had about two feet under her and calculated that the tide had only about a foot to fall. I might add that it was a warm day and, of course, I got wet up to the waist. This enabled me to get ashore to shop and make an important telephone call. If the wind had changed to an offshore breeze while I was away, I would have had to swim to the boat but this was unlikely in the extreme.

All in all, the advantages of not towing a dinghy, the better passages made and the safety in rough weather far outweigh the difficulties of getting ashore as often as the chap with a dinghy. Most of us sail small boats because we cannot afford large ones. Staying afloat is a certain way of saving money and cutting the cost of small boat cruising.

Figure 1. *Shoal Waters* under full sail on the Chelmer and Blackwater Navigation above Ulting church.

Figure 2. *Shoal Waters* sailing the Broads. Note: forestay to stemhead

Figure 3. *Shoal Waters* under storm trysail in heavy weather. Note the twin sheets on the trysail.

Figure 4. *Shoal Waters* about to navigate a gut across the mudflats about two hours after low water. There will probably be two or three feet of water in the gut.

Figure 5. Water-boots hanging on the transom of the boat, to be washed when the tide returns.

Figure 6. Cattle come down to the water's edge to greet *Shoal Waters*. We hadn't noticed them when we decided to dry there.

Figure 7. The roomy cockpit tent gives a lot more space than the tiny cabin, and privacy when needed. Excess gear from the cabin can be stowed here overnight.

Figure 8. Inside *Shoal Waters* showing the galley at the port after end of the cabin. The roll on the right is the topsail on its yard.

Figure 9. *Shoal Waters* mooring amongst the wild flowers along the Kentish Stour, where it broadens out northwards like a miniature Norfolk Broads. The tall flowers are purple wild mint.

Figure 10. *Shoal Waters* on Regent's Canal near Maida tunnel.

Figure 11. Joy and Charles Stock relaxing in the cockpit of *Shoal Waters* alongside Horning Staithe on the Norfolk Broads.

Figure 12. Beached for the night on the River Hamble, above the bridge, safe from the crowded river below.

Figure 13. *Shoal Waters* aground at Ebbsfleet near Ramsgate in 1990, ready to cross the Channel the next day for the 50th anniversary of Dunkirk.

Figure 14. *Shoal Waters* running with reefed mainsail and two headsails.

Figure 15. The author at the tiller, with QE2 astern.

Figure 16. Joy with tea.

Chapter Eleven

Kneecap Navigation

Let's be honest, my kind of navigation is not really navigation at all. Strictly speaking it is pilotage, controlling the movements of the boat by reference to visible marks on the coast, and fixed and floating marks at sea. In the absence of an elaborate chart space for Admiralty charts, I am forced to use one of the folding charts, designed for yachtsmen, balanced on my knees as I sit at the helm. It could be fairly described as map reading with water all round.

The focus of my navigation (let's use the term in its widest sense), is a fine brass binnacle compass set on the bridge deck starboard side of the hatchway. I bought it for scrap brass price, three shillings a pound. It weighed twelve pounds and cost thirty-six shillings. They were intended for motor craft. We had one on LCA 1825 (Landing Craft Assault) when I was in the Royal Marines. It was not gimballed and the card had the out of date quadrant notation. I had a new card painted with points, half points and the three sixty degree notation round the outside. Lugs were put on the bowl so that it pivots abeam but not fore and aft. When the grey paint was taken off, the brass polished up well. It is regularly sprayed with WD40 to protect it from salt water. The bowl has a glass bottom and is lit from underneath with a red filter over the bulb to help maintain night vision.

One spends a lot of time staring at the compass and I just like the look of the points card, but it has real advantages for small sailing boats. Who can steer to a degree anyway? In twelve weeks as a watch officer on the sail training schooner *Sir Winston Churchill* I have only once seen a course set that was not rounded off to the nearest five degrees. Ten degrees is nearer the mark for small boats so why not make it a full point (11.25 degrees) and have a bold point on the compass to steer by? It is just so much more interesting to steer say, south by east than one hundred and seventy degrees. You have to be able to box the compass anyway to be able to understand the reports of wind direction at local stations at the end of the Radio Four weather forecasts. That a point is an awkward 11.25 degrees is no reason for saying that the points system is old-fashioned. I suspect that it is a far newer idea than that of dividing the circle into three hundred and sixty degrees which seems to have been based on the ancient Sumerian idea that there were three hundred and sixty days in a year. The points system seems to have been of more recent Viking origin. It depends on the eye's natural ability to halve any given distance or angle. Anyway, I stick to three hundred and sixty degree notation for chart work and convert to points for use with the steering compass. For bearings I originally used a Sestrel hand bearing compass but when it became due for overhaul after twenty years faithful service, I opted for one of the newer 'pocket watch' sized bearing compasses, for the price new was little more than half that of renovating the Sestrel. On one occasion I found that the heavier Sestrel had its advantages. My boat was broken into by a chap wanted by Interpol for stealing a yacht from Hamburg. He was sailing the south coast living by stealing from boats. I don't tow a dinghy and he broke in not realising that I was on board. He looked a tough customer but after I had taken a bearing on him and swum him ashore he waited quietly enough for the police to arrive. He got six months and was deported to Germany.

When I first launched *Shoal Waters* I fixed up a Sestrel junior compass on the top of the sliding hatch at eye level so that I read it from behind. This meant minimal eye movement from the compass to the view ahead of the vessel but I found a snag. While steering north I was looking at the letter, 'N' on the southern side of the rim. As the ships head swung starboard to steer due east, the letter 'E' appeared from the left hand side. Now, I am a simple-minded soul and used to east being to the right of north and thought that there was a danger of confusion when relating the chart to the compass and vice versa when very tired. It is difficult to explain but very real and I was glad to get back to a traditional bowl compass that I viewed from above and could relate directly to a chart laid out alongside.

Deviation is the prime method for evening class instructors to bewilder their students. My advice is to put the compass where there is no appreciable deviation, i.e. not more than a degree or two, and then ignore it in your calculations. In case anyone takes exception to my casual view of one or two degrees, how many yachtsmen who cheerfully screw the compass holder to the cabin bulkhead are absolutely certain that the bulkhead is at ninety degrees to the fore and aft line of the boat? Not many I suspect. Of course it is essential to understand exactly what deviation is and how to check for it every time you leave the harbour or river. Each time I leave my mooring I steer to the middle of the river and expect Number Seven buoy to come up about south east. Only once did I find it twenty degrees out and realised that, leaving on the last of the tide, I had dumped a new cylinder of Gaz just the other side of the bulkhead from the compass. Learn the best transits on your river, mark them on your chart with bearings as seen from the compass and never miss an opportunity to check them.

With a mooring that dries out, it may be possible to walk astern of the boat when the tide is out to aim the hand bearing compass at the backstay in line with the mast, then check the reading with the steering compass for deviation. It seems to work well with bilge keel boats but not centreboarders as the plate will be up and this may affect the compass. Remember that if you are going to have a deviation card made out, you need one when sailing, one when under motor and if a centreboarder, one with the plate right up. This still leaves heeling error which will be different on each tack. If you are going to dabble with deviation, remember that if you have deviation of five degrees and ignore it you will be five degrees off course. Deviation must be added or subtracted from your magnetic course. If you get it wrong you will be *ten degrees* off course! In practice on most wooden and glass boats we find that the compass is accurate enough for local trips. My tip is to treat deviation like tuberculosis; don't worry yourself sick about it. Test regularly to see that you don't have it and then forget about it.

I like Admiralty charts but they are cumbersome on a small boat, especially if single-handed. The special yachtsmen's charts that fold are useful and once inside a river, there is a lot to be said for using the Ordinance Survey one inch maps, (Yes I know that they are now in these mysterious mid-European measurements incomprehensible to any decent honest God fearing

Englishman.) Although they don't show depths or drying heights, the shape of mud and sand exposed at low water springs is shown and this can be very useful. The mass of shore detail can help with navigation and add to the interest of the voyage. For instance an unmade road leading down to the water's edge can help to identify a disused 'farmer's landing place', as well as mud covered hards and fords. Better still but more expensive are the two and a quarter inch maps. For anyone spending a few days in Arthur Ransome's *Secret Waters* in Walton Backwaters, one of this series covers nearly the whole area and will prove an asset indeed.

I use a Douglas Protractor for chart work. The small five inch one is handier for work on folded charts in the cockpit but the ten inch model has the great advantage for middle-aged sailors with failing eyes in that the degree divisions are larger than with any other instrument available for reading off courses and putting bearings on a chart. This is purely and simply because the degree marks are further from the pivot point and thus bigger. They are so much easier to read and that must mean greater accuracy when used under stress in difficult circumstances. A piece of thread looped through the hole in the centre can be used to read off bearings without the need to write on the chart.

Keep notes of the bearings of buoys and other marks along regular routes taken when visibility is good for use in haze or fog. Get into the habit of taking a bearing on each sea mark as it comes into view in case it vanishes again for a spell while you are sailing towards it. A friend told me of a difficulty he experienced in the Spitway at night when the Wallet Spitway buoy on which he had been steering suddenly vanished. The culprit was a sand barge aground which obscured the light as they neared it. It is a local custom for these laden craft whose draft of six feet is a little more than the depth in the Spitway at low water, to just press on through until they ground and then move off as they lift with the young flood.

Perhaps the most important function of the hand bearing compass is to judge the effect of the tides across your course on your vessel. Few small boat sailors will be able to draw tidal triangles underway and have to rely on judgement, but of course the chap who has done plenty of examples at home is most likely to come up with a reasonable answer. Even if a proper computation has been made, it still needs checking for the speed of the tide can vary and, more likely, that of the boat will have been incorrectly estimated. As you leave the last mark look astern regularly. If you can line it up against the shore it is easy to find a transit. Failing this you will have to take bearings at regular intervals to see if they vary from the reciprocal of your compass course to be made good over the ground. To get a reciprocal, write one hundred and eighty under the course. Subtract if possible, if not possible, add. If it remains constant you are on course. If not you will have to adjust your heading port or starboard to get back on course. It isn't an easy problem but you only have two choices and will get it right eventually. Once the next mark comes in sight you can check the bearing with the steering compass but once again, use a transit if possible. An unlit buoy can be found by getting a crew member to stand by the mast and con the boat by watching the bearing of a properly identified light mark. Finding the Buxey Beacon in the Rays'n between the rivers Crouch and Blackwater is an interesting experiment for a warm summer night. Another use is to show that the boat is clear of a danger. Many such clearing marks are shown on charts with dangerous rocky areas, but there are few on the charts of the Thames Estuary and it is a case of making your own over the years. Sometimes I leave the Crouch in the dark and make a fast passage to the entrance to the Blackwater where I want to sleep off the rest of the ebb but stay afloat to take to next flood tide back to my mooring. I know that once the power station at Bradwell bears due west I am clear of the mud flats and can anchor for the rest of the night knowing that I will be afloat at low water. Earlier on during the same trip I know that the shallowest water is reached when the white flash of the Sunken Buxey buoy bears due east.

Do all the homework you can before the trip starts. That 'Time spent on reconnaissance is never wasted', was drummed into us during our training in the Royal Marines and it is just as true in small boat sailing. Study the charts, maps, pilot books etc. and gather together all the information you can, for you are less likely to miss vital details when sitting comfortably in an armchair than when making do with a quick glance while under way. This is never more true than when reading a chart at night by torch light. What better way to spend January evenings than planning the next season's voyages? This is where logs kept from previous voyages are so useful for the information they give on the time taken over various passages in particular conditions. The most delightful time and place for planning is in your bunk after the 0555 hrs weather forecast while drinking the first cup of tea on those days when there is no need to make an early start. Always have an alternative to the main aim in case the conditions deteriorate and never hesitate to turn back in good time. Perhaps the most important part of planning is to have information on the state and the direction of the tide to hand. The local *Admiralty Tidal Atlas* is essential among the banks of the Thames Estuary. Write in the time of high water at the standard port on the appropriate page with a soft pencil and progress backwards subtracting and forwards adding one hour per page. Then at any time during the day you can open up the little booklet to the relevant page to see what the tide is doing at that moment and flick over the pages ahead to see what is in store for you. Most important of all, it will warn of any foul tide laying in wait for you along the route.

One of the most trouble free things in navigation is the transit, i.e. when two objects well apart appear in line. Use them whenever possible, but like everything else, make certain that you identify the features correctly. Boats with coloured panels in the sails can look like beacons from a distance and upright Bermudian sails can look like cardinal marks. Anything is possible. In the old days of black and white chequered buoys I thought I spotted one on a foggy day and it turned out to be a cormorant sitting on sandbank drying its wings. Just recently the tattered black flag of a lobster pot marker seemed through the mist to be a feature on the horizon hundreds of yards away. Perhaps the biggest surprise I ever had was when approaching Lowestoft from the south and noted a large block of flats well inshore of the harbour entrance. Next time I looked the relative positions had changed. Now blocks of flats don't move but I could hardly believe our craft had moved seaward half a mile in a few minutes. A quarter of an hour later the problem was solved when the block of flats came out of the harbour entrance on a massive barge towed by two tugs, presumably on route to an oil or gas platform. As I said, anything can happen.

In areas such as the Thames it is far easier to find your way about at night as most of the buoys are lit and easier to identify than by daylight. In 1951 I worked my way into Kings Lynn from Hunstanton on a rising tide after dark by following the buoys listed in *Reed's Almanac*. In those days *Reeds* only cost five shillings, (the price of seven loaves of sliced bread.) The only 'chart' I had was the quarter inch road map of the area and I just couldn't find the Roaring Middle light vessel. Next day I found it in Kings Lynn being repainted. Seven by fifty binoculars are essential for night sailing, although I can remember the days before I could afford them but then my eyes were young. As we grow older, and our vision fades we tend to be wealthier which is just as well. A teenage lookout on *Malcolm Miller* brought this home to me when I found he could pick out lights with his naked eye as early as I could find them with binoculars. Buy the type with individual adjustment for each eye rather than those with centre focusing as they are more waterproof. If you are flush, buy glasses filled with nitrogen which are totally safe from the elements. Once you have got them set for your eyes, Sellotape them for you will not be able to readjust them in the dark if they move. Lastly don't rely on your sense of direction for there just ain't no such animal! Even more important, don't be diverted from your carefully thought-out decisions by the sense of direction of others on board, however loudly they proclaim them. Trust the chart and your compass. They are the best crew members you will ever have.

Chapter Twelve

Constructing a Cruise

One of the most bewildering aspects of yachting in the eighties is the mass of boats in every marina and mooring area and the few boats one meets actually sailing up and down the coast. Some people are content to stay in their home river and a number regard boats as something to work on rather than for sailing. Others clearly regard owning a boat as the prestigious thing to do. One chap owned a fast modern vessel that conformed to the Junior Offshore Group rules. He kept her at Maldon and insured her for cruising and racing between the Elbe and Le Havre. His home was packed with sailing books and he would pontificate on sailing matters for evermore including regular contributions in the correspondence columns of the yachting press. I believe that he had once sailed as far as Harwich and been involved in a big insurance claim. In the ten years that I knew him, to the best of my knowledge, he never sailed out of the river. There remains a substantial body of small boat owners who would like to get about more but somehow never quite manage it. Learning to sail has never been easier. There have never been more gadgets and go-fast goodies on the market to help the boat along. The difficulty of learning to *cruise* remains. Undoubtedly the concentration on racing light dinghies when young and the total neglect of seamanship is an important factor. How often one sees the racing man buy a cruiser once his family comes along and set off down the river confident that this branch of the sport is easy after the cut and thrust of racing. Suddenly he finds himself up the creek without a paddle and it dawns on him that the sideboard at home groaning under the weight of chromium plated crockery is no use in this game. By the time he picks up his mooring again, his wife and family have been scared out of their lives and put off sailing for years, perhaps for ever. It could be so different with careful planning and preparation.

Don't be too ambitious. Aim to reach out a little further than you have done before but also have alternatives if conditions are unfavourable. Remember the old formula for one third of your time outward bound and two thirds to get home again. You can always shorten the outward trip but will have no choice on the length of the trip home. Take a careful look at the chart of the Thames Estuary. You will see that for the small cruiser it divides up into three areas; the Medway and Southend area, the Crouch, Blackwater and Colne area and the Harwich area. Once within each area the small cruiser can move about freely in reasonable weather. Travelling from one area to the next is more difficult and at times impossible for days on end. The twelve miles between Colne Point and the Naze is an easy leap with a fair wind but taxes the windward ability of small cruisers when the wind comes ahead. Don't delude yourself that as the coast curves from due east to due north the wind cannot be on the nose all the way. It can, particularly early in the day for the southbound boat when the wind veers with the sun. The secret is to start in good time. The southbound vessel should be off Walton Pier by the time the tide begins to flood and the northbound one off Colne point when the ebb sets in. High water at Colne Point is half an hour later than at the Naze. The northbound vessel looses thirty minutes of fair tide and the southbound one gains the same amount. This works out fairly well as the latter presumably wants to take the last of the flood tide on into one of the rivers, while the northbound vessel is glad to find the new flood helping him into Harwich. Incidentally, if you do find yourself outside Harwich with a northerly wind and plenty of ebb left to run, you can usually anchor comfortably in the lee of the breakwater for a meal.

The trip from the Spitway to Sea Reach in the Thames is an altogether more formidable problem. It's a much longer trip and the seas will get a lot rougher. There is not much relief to be found by easing sheets for the East Swale, for you still have to beat in when you get there. Cutting over Foulness Sands is out of the question if you want to work the tides for the sands will be uncovered by the time you are at the Whittaker having brought the ebb out of the Crouch ready to take the flood into the Thames. I have gritted my teeth and bashed on over the tide but it can be a long, hard trip and is to be avoided if possible. Nevertheless, all is not gloom. The small boat owner has a joker in his hand; the ancient creek at Havengore, literally the Haven by the Gore. It separates Foulness Island from the mainland. The one bridge only lifts for boats at weekends as this area is a busy firing range during the rest of the week. It is only available around high water when there is six feet over the sands at springs and three at neaps. This inevitably means problems working the tides and it is probably more use to the vessel bound north which can cross the miles of shallow sands while they are covering. Once through the bridge he will find plenty of water along the creeks that lead to the rivers Roach and Crouch and a fair tide to help him on his way. Over the years I suspect that many yachtsmen have been put off this route by the name of the final channel that leads to the bridge. It is called Narrow Cuts. Any doubts that may have existed in their minds about the amount of water in this channel for their small cruiser was finally scotched by the passage in July 1986 of the centre section for the new bridge on a large lighter, towed by a tug drawing four feet eight inches, two hours before high water neaps. On the other hand the southbound yacht can reach the bridge at least an hour or two before high water but will then have to wait for the sands to cover. Once through, she will have three miles of shallow sand to cover before reaching deep water, by which time the tide will be ebbing strongly.

If you plan to go further afield, for instance to the Broads or the south coast it is just not possible to rely on suitable weather for the passage at the start of a holiday. Watch for a fair wind over the previous three or four weekends and make the trip whenever the chance occurs, leaving the boat there ready for your holiday. I did this to make certain of a Broads holiday several times, covering the seventy miles in fifteen to twenty hours on my own. Once when we visited the South coast I split the trip in half: a thirty-four hour trip to Rye and seventeen hours for the rest of the trip to Bembridge a week later.

If the weather allows, try for a bold start. There is a lot to be said for making a night passage after work on Friday, for you are unlikely to sleep well the first night on board and the magic of arriving somewhere new, early on the first day, sets the seal on a successful holiday. There is a lot to be said for keeping your options open so that you get a fair wind to start the holiday. In other words, sail down to the river mouth and let the wind decide whether you turn north or south. During the rest of the holiday I find we don't do much night sailing for it means sleeping at least part of the next day. Watch the weather forecast several days before the holiday starts and never miss a forecast during the holiday if you can help it. Get in tune with the tides and have a list of the times of high water made out and displayed prominently on board together with the times of sunrise, sunset, moon rise and moon set. During unsettled weather sail early in the day to snatch a passage before the wind strengthens. In any case it is always a good thing to have plenty of daylight in hand. It always pays to 'have a look at it' provided that you can get back into shelter easily. Many a time I have found it rougher in the river than outside. When it is rough, reef down and get at least a little sailing inside the river if at all possible. Take advantage of light weather to voyage out round the banks.

Chapter Thirteen

The One Ton Weekend Cruise

However successful the annual holiday cruise may or may not be, the season's sailing inevitably revolves round the weekend trip. It provides the perfect antidote to the stress and frustration of the working week. Odds and ends of statistics surface occasionally to show how many people have been drowned from small boats, but no one can come up with the total number of people whose sanity in this cockeyed world is dependant on the therapeutic benefits of the hours they spend afloat in small boats. The chap who had the scare of his life (until next time) in the Wallet last Saturday will ride the petty feuds in the office or factory as buoyantly as his little ship rode those gigantic waves in that yachtsman's gale off Clacton pier. Stress is a most worrying health problem today; sea time in small boats is the complete cure.

Most owners of small cruisers accept that the paramount need to be back home on Sunday evening limits the weekend trip to a modest voyage to the river mouth. This suits many people but others crave something more exciting. The East Anglian Offshore Racing Association has excitement galore to offer and is always short of crews. I sailed with them in the post-war years. Most of the boats were pre-war and the one I usually crewed on, a *Clyde*

Thirty dated from Edwardian times. Today the best of modern yacht design is to be found in the fleet and everything is taken much more seriously, far too seriously for me. The last race I did was the traditional August Bank holiday race from Harwich to Ostend. While relaxing in Ostend yacht basin it occurred to me that we had joined the boat, a *Stella,* at Wolverstone on Thursday evening, raced the ninety miles to Ostend on Friday and would return home on Tuesday or Wednesday. This gave just one hundred and eighty miles of sailing in five or six days. Forgetting for a moment that the work was divided among a crew of four, this comes out at just under forty miles a day, less that I was averaging in my old half-decker *Zephy*r. My time afloat was limited by the demands of a growing family and as a farm bailiff on an arable farm, my season ended when the combine harvester started to roll. There must be a way to spend a higher proportion of my leisure actually underway. Why not sail a small cruiser with the same spirit and determination one finds aboard the offshore fleet! Of course it would not be possible to press on regardless when the weather said 'No', but this could be more than made good by the freedom to sail wherever the wind suggested, rather than stick to a race programme drawn up at the start of the season. My thoughts went back to 1961 and my first trip out of the river in *Zephyr* since 1953. It was a sudden decision prompted by the ribald remarks made about her by my fellow club members when she was brought ashore up the new club ramp. In fairness it must be admitted that she looked a sad sight against the gleaming varnished dinghies and I felt the need to redeem her. A fortnight later I sailed with the early morning ebb to the river mouth and picked up the flood up the Swin to cross the Maplin sands into Havengore Creek, under the lifting bridge, to moor overnight in the Crouch and return home next day, a round trip of some sixty miles. The magic of small boat cruising gripped me once more. What was more important, I had been at the helm for those sixty miles. Let me explain that this was before the days of self steering. Everyone wanted to steer. Those who couldn't be prised off the helm without resorting to gunpowder were labelled 'Helm Hogs'. Even today, Joy has to demand her share of time at the tiller on *Shoal Waters*. A very frail elderly lady still comes down to the club on quiet weekdays. I never meet her without thinking of the time in the early fifties when a fellow crew member, seeing her aboard another yacht in Heybridge lock said. 'She is a dammed good crew *but*, she's a helm hog!'

What stuck in my mind about my trip up the Swin was how leisurely it had been. Visibility had been good. The Isle of Sheppey stood out clearly and I was struck by the fact that I could easily have reached Medway by high water. Thus *Shoal Waters* was built to do the trip out from Heybridge, round the Isle of Sheppey and get home again between my leaving work on Friday and sunset on Sunday. From here it was an easy leap to conceive the idea of the one ton weekend trip.

Look at it this way. It is some twelve or thirteen miles from Heybridge lock to the Bench Head buoy at the river mouth. The voyage down with the ebb, round the buoy and home with the flood is done each season by hundreds of local craft well within the twelve hour period between high tides, leaving plenty of time for lunch off Bradwell or West Mersea and tea at Osea. Local dinghies race for the 'Rum Tub and Bung' over this route each year. Thus a twenty-five mile trip between one high water and the next, twelve hours later is simple enough. Pack four such trips into the weekend and there is your one hundred mile trip. Obviously it needs much more planning but the logistics are straightforward. Over the years ninety-nine per cent of my trips average out better than three knots but well under four knots made good. At this rate a hundred mile trip will mean about thirty hours sailing. With high water roughly an hour later each day this gives us some fifty hours of potentially fair tide each weekend, leaving nearly twenty hours for eating sleeping and just lazing about. At Heybridge we dry for some six hours every tide but I do not find this a serious snag as I need the ebb tide down the River Blackwater anyway.

The weather is the final arbiter and will dictate which trips, if any, are possible. Watch the weather pattern from Wednesday onwards to get an idea of the trend. Sail as soon as possible after leaving work on Friday afternoon. Aim to be wherever you are going by noon on Saturday and complete a substantial part of the return trip before anchoring for a sound night's sleep on Saturday. Remember the basic rule for cruising in our fickle climate: one third of your time outward bound and two thirds to get back home. I do not suggest that you need do this sort of trip every weekend but when you do, the sheer satisfaction of a good passage will send you back to the office on Monday morning feeling on top of the world.

After an article in a leading yachting journal the above philosophy was challenged by a correspondent who said that it was out of the question in our climate to sail to somewhere thirty miles away on Saturday and return on Sunday regularly without an engine. It was a challenge that I couldn't resist. Total mileage each season varied between one thousand two hundred and one thousand seven hundred miles. The idea was to make an early start and cover five hundred miles by Easter. If this could be achieved it would be possible to top two thousand miles for the season. *Shoal Waters* was refitted early that year and launched the last Sunday in January into a smooth sea under a warm sun. It was a good omen for a season which I have never bettered.

			Miles
February:	1/2	Shake down cruise to river mouth	25
	8/9	Colne Point	30
	14/16	Battlesbridge	70
	22/23	Rochford	70
March:	1/2	Round Buxey Sand and West Mersea	63
	7/9	Stow Maries Creek	67
	15/16	Battlesbridge	84
	21/24	Pin Mill, Manningtree, Walton and round East Barrow Sand	116
Easter:		Rochester, Havengore by night and Clacton	130
April:	4/6	NE Gunfleet buoy and Burnham	90
	19/20	Stow Maries and Havengore	74
	25/27	Hole Haven, round Isle of Sheppey	120
May:	3/4	Roughs Tower, Fambridge and Rochford	120
	10/12	Colne and Brightlingsea	47

			Miles
	17/19	Walton, Harwich and Havengore	96
Bank Holiday:		Chelmsford canal	30
June:	31/1	Aldeburgh and Walton	101
	7/8	Queenborough and Burnham	103
	13/15	Woodbridge	100
	22/23	Black Deep, Havengore, Fambridge	105
	28/29	Ipswich, Walton and Colne	114
July:	5/6	Fen Creek Havengore, Barrow Deep and Allresford (Colne)	114
	11/12	Round Bridgemarsh, Rochford	88
	26/27	Old Gaffers Race	49
August:	2/3	Sea lavender cruise to Hoo Outfall	32
	8/10	West Mersea, BSC regatta, Colne and Spitway	70
	15/17	Havengore and Spitway	64
Holiday:		Clipper Regatta, Hampden Court, Rochester and Harwich	329
September:	6/7	Havengore	65
	13/14	Brightlingsea, Bradwell	42
	19/21	Medway, Battlesbridge, Colne	130
	26/28	Bradwell, Spitway	52

			Miles
October:	4/6	Round Rushley and Potton Islands	64
	11/12	Battlesbridge	72
	17/19	Walton, Manningtree, Pyefleet	106
November:	8/10	Colchester	45
	14/16	West Mersea, Salcot cum Virley	35
	22/23	Bridgemarsh	54
	29/31	West Mersea and Stow Creek (fog)	64
December:	13/17	Burnham, Brightlingsea in fog and frost	65
Total miles covered during 1977 season			3307

Let me be honest and admit that I have never repeated the experiment above for, as I feared when I set out, sailing to maximise distance sailed is almost as bad as racing for destroying the sheer joy of cruising under sail. To the best of my knowledge it is an unbeaten achievement and proof indeed of the potential of a small and inexpensive boat designed to sail the Thames Estuary. It took me several years to get back to sailing just for the sheer pleasure of feeling the tiller alive in my hand and to visit most of the area each year for the sheer joy of doing so.

Chapter Fourteen

September Cruise

Saturday 28 August found me facing the glorious prospect of eight days of solo freedom aboard *Shoal Waters* with no special event, race or other fixture demanding my attendance at a certain place at a predetermined time. All I wanted to do was to sail and sail and sail. Each daylight high water would find me at the head of a different river or creek. Which rivers and creeks, and in what sequence they would be explored, would depend entirely on the whims of the wind.

The first high water was at 0532 hrs. When I left my mooring an hour earlier there was a useful breeze from the south-west under a clear sky. As my little ship headed south-east, past the marooned remnants of the broken sea walls fringing flooded Northey Island, the great constellation of Orion stood out boldly between the mast and the starboard shrouds, a sure sign of the imminence of Autumn. A barge at anchor off Osea Island and the usual cluster of riding lights on yachts moored east of the decaying old pier completed a perfect send off. When the wind fell light off Bradwell I took the chance to brew up, ready to plan the day's sport in the light of the shipping forecast at 0630 hrs. By the time it came over giving SW5/6 for the Thames area, I was halfway to the Bench Head buoy at the river mouth with the wind already rising. A glance astern in the first light of dawn showed several other craft on the same route including a barge, presumably the one I had seen off Osea Pier.

The sun appeared soon after seven o'clock over a bank of clouds and twenty minutes later I reefed the mainsail right down but hung onto full jib (still sloop rigged at this time). Other craft reefed, ran under jib only or even under engine. I decided that the sooner I was into Harwich the better, although in fact earlier I had been toying with the idea of Lowestoft. Clacton Pier drew abeam at 0750 hrs, followed by the usual headlong rush to Walton at 0845 hrs. In the shelter of the Naze I set the smaller jib and got well over into the lee of the rapidly uncovering Pye Sand. There was a barge well ahead, seeming to have come round the north-east Gunfleet and another, the *Dawn* of Maldon, well out to seaward, was catching up fast. At 0950 hrs we passed into Harwich in brilliant sunshine. My commiserations went to some club members heading south on the Crusader class *Tamarisk*, and obviously in for a rough time. There was now time aplenty to visit Ipswich ten miles up the River Orwell at high water, so I anchored under the Shotley shore at 1020 hrs for breakfast and a nap. It seemed to be a popular idea for many other craft gathered off Stoneheaps during the next hour or two, including three barges.

While I eventually moved on up river the wind was more westerly for I couldn't quite point the course. After shopping at Pin Mill I sailed up to the first road bridge at Ipswich under heavy skies on a dreary afternoon. The 1800 hrs forecast gave a gale warning for Thames, SW 5/6/7 ñ eight later. This cancelled my plans to lay off Stoneheaps for the night with a view to carrying on to Southwold or

Lowestoft next day and I moored on the western mud at Pin Mill soon afterwards to bed down early for a full night's sleep.

Away at 0640 hrs in a dreary purple dawn with a light breeze from the south-west that hardened as I left the shelter of the trees and high ground. The forecast repeated the gale warning but said that the wind would decrease later. It was no day for a long coastal passage but I decided to slip round into the Deben, just five miles north of Harwich, rounding Colimer Point at 0710 hrs for a steady beat out of the harbour at 0815 hrs. A big Baltic ketch leaving at the same time interested me. He left the starboard hand Beach End buoy to starboard and then cut back across the curving shipping channel to leave the next port hand buoy to port, shouting to me at the same time that I was going the wrong side of the buoys. Then a ferry came in and he realised his mistake! The sun came out and I had a pleasant run into the Deben over the ebb, cutting the corner safely and anchored closed alongside the steep shingle bank inside the first sheltered bend below the ferry. This gave me a chance to watch the dinghy types getting their boats down the steep shingle bank into the water and even help a *Hornet* back up the shingle when a stone jammed her plate. As I suspected, it was very hard work indeed.

The sun soon left us and it turned cold for the rest of the day. At Ramsholt I met some people in a red *Falcon* who were delighted to see *Shoal Waters*. They came aboard for the trip up to Woodbridge with me and it made a pleasant trip, during which I showed them how to put in and take out a reef with the old-fashioned points and cringles.

Woodbridge on a bank holiday Sunday was almost like a trip back into the thirties with crowds on the promenade and the local band playing in the bandstand. On the way back I spotted Ronald Simper and after I dropped the Falcon types, I ran back for a meal and to look over his latest boat, the Swedish Pilot Cutter *L'Atalanta*. It was long after dark when we finished yarning and I anchored for the night in the shelter of the trees at the Rocks.

Bank holiday Monday greeted me with a perfect summer sunrise over the trees and a forecast of winds west, north-west force four to five. This would be an offshore wind on the tricky Ore Bar giving an easy admission to the glorious fifteen miles of rural Suffolk past Orford and Aldeburgh to the first bridge at Snape. The entrance known ominously as Shingle Street, is only five miles along the coast but the ebb runs at up to seven knots and entrance is not normally possible until near or after low water, so there was no hurry to leave the River Deben. This bright sunshine and warm breeze was too good to miss so I sailed upstream over the ebb to Waldringfield, glad of the chance to get some colour slides of this delightful east facing waterfront in sunshine for it is normally in shade for most of the day. These were as pleasant conditions as one could wish for sailing and I beat on upstream as far as the Woodbridge YC before turning back for a glorious run down river with the ebb. After the usual hectic few moments in the turmoil on the bar at 1050 hrs I turned north and was surprised to see from the lobster pots that the tide was already going south. Nevertheless it was still pouring out of the Ore at Shingle Street an hour later. My tactic to dodge the surf on the bar by using a shallow channel close inshore was greeted by a hail of shingle thrown by beach fishermen, a sad event on such a lovely day.

My good humour was restored off the southern point of Havergate Island where I found the old eight metre *Pleiades of Rhu*. She had been immortalised in Ian Rutherford's book *At The Tiller*, which told of bold cruising in the wild waters of western Scotland and across to Norway after her racing days were over. Now in her old age she was enjoying more leisurely waters. They asked me the depth in the entrance to the Butley river and I went ahead with the sounding pole to guide them in, big ship style. Just above Orford I found an enormous web aerial, complete with its own atomic power station, being built on the shingle spit. It spread for acres with hundreds of pylons and what must have been hundreds of miles of wire. Tales were already circulating that it would cause sparks to jump out of transistor radios up to three miles out to sea. Rumour has it that when they switched it on, it didn't work and it has now been largely removed, leaving a just few pylons which broadcast the BBC World Service. After anchoring for a lazy lunch I pressed on with the flood to the old maltings at Snape at 1615 hrs as light rain began to fall, leaving again at 1845 hrs to moor for the night at the Oaks a mile downstream. The sun showed herself briefly at sunset, flooding the glorious Suffolk countryside with a rich golden glow. Having turned in so early I was wide awake at 0200 hrs and made a cup of tea to drink during a session picking out the constellations and stars in what was now a clear velvet sky, with the aid of a book by Patrick Moore.

Tuesday's bright sunrise didn't last and light clouds covered the sky by the time I sailed for Aldeburgh and the inevitable shopping mid morning before dropping down river with the ebb. Orford, with its ancient quay, red brick warehouse, church and castle keep looked as attractive as ever in the warm sunshine, as the fierce tide swept past.

Below Havergate Island the shingle spit on the seaward side narrows quickly and the roar of the surf comes across clearly to wet one's appetite for the inevitable rough and tumble on the bar still two miles away. Once over the bar at 1220 hrs with the wind force three to four from the west, I stood out to sea on starboard tack for a long, long wait for the Cork Light Vessel to swing with the flood tide. The 1400 hrs forecast gave NW 4/5 going west, then south-west later in the Thames area. With the first of the flood I tacked over to the Platters Sand and then south past the wreck (long since removed) to get the best of the west bound tide into the Walton Backwaters where I anchored against the mud flats opposite the Stone at 1700 hrs. Unfortunately there were all the signs of a heavy cold coming on. After a meal I took the rest of the flood tide down Hamford Water, looked into Oakley Creek and then one of the shallow creeks opposite Kirby Creek that were staked off when the Oakley explosives factory was built before the first world war. The wide meres beyond were smothered with birds as the sun went down. This was by far the best sunset of the holiday so far and I followed the Maurice Griffiths *Swan* route into Landmere for the night from my copy of *Magic of the Swatchways*. As I anchored in the dying light the magic was destroyed by the arrival of a small sailing yacht under motor who did a complete circle round me before anchoring almost alongside.

Sure enough I woke with a heavy cold next morning. In bright sunshine I sailed round into Kirby Creek meeting an *Atalanta* bound out. In fact we were both bound for the Walton and Frinton YC to moor up for a shopping expedition. Her safe, deep water route would take her back to Stone Point to get into the Walton channel. *Shoal Waters* worked her way up Kirby Creek and over the wide shallow

Wade south of Horsey Island to join the main channel close to the town, where an elderly gentleman commented that she was the first craft he had seen reach the club at the head of the shallow creek under sail for a long time. When I returned to the boat with my shopping, including Profoc the current instant cold cure, the *Atalanta* was moored alongside the popular club wharf ahead of *Shoal Waters*.

'Didn't we meet you going into Kirby creek?'

Then I sailed back to the Dardanells, a deep but unfashionable mooring opposite Walton Stone, to anchor and sleep off my cold. I was entertained by some dozen youngsters, who had been camping 'Swallows and Amazons' style on Horsey Island. A motor cruiser had arrived to take them and their gear back to civilisation. She arrived at high water but instead of coming right into the creek, she laid off Stone Point five hundred yards away. All their gear was ferried out to her in a rubber duck. Inevitably there was a lot of it, which meant many journeys. The falling tide soon revealed an ever widening band of soft mud through which every load had to be carried. Each time the dinghy returned the mud was wider and softer. Gradually everything and everybody became covered in black mud. It was nearly low water by the time the final party left. One young lady struggling out through the knee deep mud with a heavy pack, stumbled backwards and sat down with both arms in the mud over her elbows.

'I hate this place,' she screamed.

The 1800 hrs' forecast brought a gale warning of SW 5/7 decreasing 4/6. That evening I sailed round the Twizzle, went ashore for a look at the marina under construction there and then crossed the Wade to Kirby Creek for the night. Before turning in I took a stroll to the top of the bird watcher's tower on Skipper's Island.

Thursday came in bright but distinctly cool. The 0630 hrs forecast was W 4/5 going SW 5/6 and I left twenty minutes later under full sail, in two minds about a trip down the coast but settled for a trip to Beaumont Quay, towing up the canal from the south bank in warm sunshine. Sheer perfection! After breakfast alongside the venerable stones of the quay that were once part of Old London Bridge, built in 1176, I sailed out through the original channel, whose winding ways had caused the canal to be dug in the first place, and worried my way round the back of the Skipper's Island and crossed the Wade again. After a stop at the Stone for a coffee and to sink my toes into the soft sand while I toyed with the idea of swimming and giving the boat a scrub, the sight of the barge *Thalatta* leaving Harwich lured me south. There was still enough water for *Shoal Waters* to slip through the gut and beat close inshore round the Naze out of the ebb tide to reach Walton Pier at 1335 hrs. Of course I had to go out into the ebb tide to get round the pier, but although I left plenty of room for the lines of the fisherman, one character dropped a heavy lead six feet behind me. I went inshore, and after anchoring in water waist deep so that the boat did not dry before I got back, telephoned the police but they wouldn't take it seriously. Having got wet, I scrubbed the boat before having a meal and listening to the 1400 hrs forecast W SW 4/5. Under way again at 1505 hrs I put in a long tack to seaward across a smooth sea but the wind was shifting about and it went round when I eventually came about so that I had made little progress by the time I closed the shore again. By the 1800 hrs forecast I was close to Clacton Pier with cloud building up in the south. It gave W4/5. The wind was rising and I pulled down a reef. There were many other craft about, mostly beating south. *Thalatta* brailed her mainsail and continued under motor as I made a long leg to the Spitway. Visibility improved rapidly and by 1830 hrs I could see both the Knoll and the Wallet Spitway buoys on a clear hard horizon. Just for the hell of it I decided to go through the Spitway and beat down the Whittaker Channel to the River Crouch in the dark. It was 1930 hrs when I reached the Swin Spitway buoy and lit the navigation lamps, steering SSW now. My cold seemed to have gone and I was getting my second wind for sailing. The moon, nearly full, came up away to the south-east as the wind eased and the sea smoothed out once more. The reef came out at 2000 hrs. Forty-five minutes later the Ridge buoy appeared in the track of moonlight and I noted that there was now plenty of tide in my favour. The Sunken Buxey buoy swept by at 0020 hrs under a beautiful silvery moon while my attention focused on some strange lights over by the Ray yellow buoy. A motor boat seemed to be helping a sailing craft. After all, this was Burnham week and boats regularly get stranded dodging the ebb tide. The wind had gone NW by the time I reached the river mouth and anchored in the lee of the outfall beacon.

A glorious canopy of stars looked down mockingly when I woke at 0330 hrs, for *Shoal Waters* was already aground and thus unable to take the last of the ebb tide out to the Whittaker Beacon to pick up the flood into the Thames. To add to my dismay the 0600 hrs forecast was W 3/4. If only I had had the guts to press on over the sands last night! I sailed as soon as she floated at 0710 hrs under a grey sky with a hint of drizzle, setting the big jib as a spinnaker and keeping well over to the northern side of the channel to dodge the flood tide until I was well past the Sunken Buxey buoy at 0830 hrs. At 0900 hrs I set the big jib to port and headed across the channel steering SE. The wind was rising now and the big jib came in at 0920 hrs by which time the Knock John Gun Tower and the West Barrow Beacon were in transit to port. I beat on over the first of the ebb but the wind began to ease and at 1205 hrs I anchored north of the Blacktail Spit as I could no longer make any useful progress. The wind died completely for the long afternoon during which I slept and later walked over the sands to one of the Blacktail Beacons.

A light breeze encouraged me to get under way at 1650 hrs steering SSW on starboard tack but the last of the ebb soon swept me well to the east. The North Oaze crept passed to port at 1730 hrs and I got the lights set up as the 1800 hrs forecast gave SW to W 2/4. Fifteen minutes later off the East Spile I spotted something big coming up from the east. The glasses showed it to be the cruiser HMS *Belfast* being towed up to the Pool of London where she has become a permanent exhibition of Britain's naval traditions. My mind flashed back to Boxing day 1943 and my leaving the office after dark to see on the placards that the battle cruiser *Scharnhorst*, the pride of the German navy, had been sunk off North Cape in the last sea battle in which ships were able to get on with the job without interference from the air. A key factor in the battle had been a six inch shell from *Belfast* which knocked out the German's forward radar so that she stumbled blindfold into the fifteen inch guns of the battleship *Duke of York*. I tacked across to meet her and got some cherished colour slides in the gloom of an overcast evening. When I reached the Medway buoy at 1935 hrs there was plenty of flood tide in my favour but no commercial traffic about, so I tacked down the main shipping channel between the twinkling port and starboard hand buoys passed the wartime wreck of the explosives laden liberty ship *Richard Montgomery* towards the lights on the Isle of Grain power station site. As I swept thorough the entrance to the Medway at 2115 hrs the moon was peeping out from behind the clouds and soon the whole sky cleared. Now with the wind free *Shoal Waters* enjoyed glorious sailing in smooth water before lowering down for Kingsferry bridge at 2230 hrs. There was more breeze where the channel turned south past lonely Elmley Island, with the stink of local industry in the air, as she tore on through the broad waters of the East Swale. It was difficult to judge the distance from the low sea walls along the shore but I was able to pick out the few channel buoys with my glasses. Great flocks of sea birds rose up into the moonlight as I approached them. Off Conyer Creek the 0030 hrs forecast gave Dover SW 2/4 and I anchored for the night just west of the moorings at Harty Ferry as the rising mist became fog and closed in around me.

The fog was really thick when I looked out next morning. High water on Saturday was at 1246 hrs, so I decided to take the opportunity to visit the lovely old port of Faversham, just a few miles away, which left plenty of time for the mist to clear before I set off along the winding creek past the old wharves and warehouses to arrive at 1215 hrs. There was little wind when I left an hour later for a slow trip to the entrance at 1450 hrs but the sun was out now and a blue sea was littered with yachts enjoying a light breeze from the north-east. It was obviously going to be a slow passage back across the Thames and I began to worry about an early return of the fog for visibility was already bad. While drinking a cup of tea at 1710 hrs off the Middle Sands I looked up to find that visibility had suddenly improved dramatically for I could see the Essex shore, including the installations on Foulness Island, in vivid detail. A strawberry moon came up in the east as I crossed the northernmost shipping lane at 1920 hrs near the East Maplin buoy. At 2055 hrs my plate touched the Maplin Sands and *Shoal Waters* was in home waters again, altering course north-east along the edge of the sands until they covered sufficiently for her to cut across to the Whittaker Channel. By 2110 hrs the white flash of the Sunken Buxey was visible due north. When the wind died at 2145 hrs I anchored for a little sleep but it soon filled in from the east and I pressed on in silver moonlight at 2350 hrs. The little boat was going like a train as she passed the Sunken Buxey buoy at 0025 hrs to storm up the Rays'n, and turn into the River Blackwater at 0130 hrs to anchor at 0300 hrs for a long sleep before taking the Sunday flood tide to her mooring.

Shoal Waters had sailed two hundred and fifty miles in nine days.

Chapter Fifteen

Summer Cruise

Over the winter months I had conducted some careful and crafty negotiations to persuade my wife to let me take two weeks holiday on my own this summer, for although the boat had proved herself at weekend sailing, *Shoal Waters* had yet to make a really good cruise. The holiday was fixed for 5 June 1965 for two weeks to cover the period of the full moon, and I spent many a pleasant hour in glorious contemplation and planning. The Solent certainly has its attractions and another trip round to the Wash would be delightful, but with these long voyages there is always the danger of getting bottled up in small harbours for days on end by bad weather. *Shoal Waters* was designed for the Thames Estuary and there is certainly a fortnight's sailing there by any standards. Most of the rivers and estuaries can provide at least some sailing under conditions when it is too rough for coastal passages. My eventual plan was to explore the traditional trade routes of this historic area, sweeping through the Swin in time-honoured fashion when wind and tides served, then delving deep into the heart of the Kent, Essex and Suffolk countryside to wherever a derelict wharf or mill showed that men once traded there under sail. I was particularly keen to explore the River Stour above Sandwich in Kent. The one inch OS map that I had kept from my days with the Royal Marines showed this area to be very similar to the Norfolk Broads, with few houses near the river, but I could find no trace of anyone having sailed there. Lastly, I had the idea of exploring the Thames as far as London Bridge but preferred to leave this until the end of the trip in case of accidents among all the traffic. Above all things, my aim was to spend as much time as possible sailing and as little as possible on shore. Food and gear was stowed to this end and every detail, down to such considerations as trimming my nails was carried out.

Most of the gear was put on board during the week so that when I got on board on Friday all I had to take was hand gear too valuable to leave on board such as the radio, camera and binoculars and a new boom tent which had just been made for me by my local sailmaker. It was just five o'clock in the afternoon, the sun was shining, the wind SE 3/4 going light and southerly and it took me just fifteen minutes to get underway and set off with the ebb tide precisely at high water. The obvious plan was to start the holiday by calling in on the Southend Barge Race at 1030 hrs next morning. Osea Pier slipped by at 1815 hrs and I made a cup of tea in the shelter of the Stansgate shore. In fact, I was in no hurry for once but I never miss a chance of a brew up, for one never knows when the next chance will occur. Starboard tack took me out to the Nass Beacon off West Mersea, then a port tack to Sales Point and after another board to the Mersea shore I came about and found I could point the Buxey Beacon. There was chill in the air and a newish moon showed boldly over the lonely sea wall defending the fertile marshes of the Denghie Hundred. By 2100 hrs I could pick out the Sunken Buxey buoy in the Whittaker Channel but, of course, there was a lot of very shallow water to traverse before I got there. I had read of the two buoys put down by the joint Burnham clubs to mark the Ray Sand Channel and found them easily, a yellow spherical about a mile north of the shallowest part and a white spherical on the tail of the Buxey Sand just south of the shallows. I sounded through into deep water at 2150 hrs. Now came the decision, either to go out round the Whittaker and down the Swin with all the danger of fog in steamer lanes or to go through the channels to Havengore and thus out onto the Thames at high water. The inside passage is more trouble but it is so much safer for so much longer and that is the one I took. Just before midnight I was almost rammed by a yacht under motor in the River Crouch, presumably because the helmsman was blinded by the bright lights inside the cabin as he had the doors wide open. I bellowed at the top of my voice and he swung away at the last moment. My navigation lights stood out plainly enough for him to have seen, had he been keeping a proper lookout. It was half an hour after midnight when I got to the Middleway. The channel was very narrow and a long spit of mud stretched out from Rushley Island but there was depth enough once I found it. I was very early on the tide and as the wind had died right away for the moment, I lowered the sails, pulled the rudder onto the afterdeck and let her drift with the swirling current between the silent banks of mud topped by saltings and sea walls. Now and again the stern or bows would touch the mud and the boat would swing round and hesitate for a minute or two before continuing on towards the bridge. I snatched the chance for a snack and hot drink. It was important for me to reach the bridge while the tide was still sweeping out towards the sands as they do not open it at night and I would have to go under with the mast lowered when it is difficult for me to manoeuvre. I was under by 0315 hrs and had a hard beat over the shallow sands by the Orwell Beacon in light easterly airs for, of course, my plate was almost completely up and by the time that the water was deep enough to cross, the tide was flowing towards the bridge. Gradually I made enough ground to be able to let the plate down a little and then progress improved, so that I began to get the benefit of the flood tide down the coast. It was just light enough to take a colour slide as I reached the defence boom and it came out showing the light marking the half tide gap actually flashing. From here I could see the outline of many barges over near the pier, but it was a long, slow sail to reach them, west of the pier at 0705 hrs by which time it was nearly flat calm.

A little sleep, a wash and then breakfast. The forecast was light north-east but it eventually came in south-east much later in the day. I got underway just before grounding, as the ten minute gun for the race sounded. It was a sad slow start and I left them to hurry across to the Medway in order to get into the river before the flood began to carry me up the Thames. At noon I was off the Nore Swatch and put up the spinnaker to gather the faint breeze from the north-east. I passed between the forts guarding the Medway at 1200 hrs. Other craft about me were using their engines, *Shoal Waters* kept moving through the water in her steady relentless manner that breaks the hearts of other small cruiser owners. The large fort on the Sheppey shore is massive and part of it is now used by the coast guard and harbour control. The Grain Fort over on the western side is much smaller, in fact it stands well out into the river and is deserted these days, even the causeway that joined it to the sea wall has collapsed. Chatham was a fleet base for hundreds of years, and fortifications cover the whole estuary.

Darnet Ness Fort passed to port and Hoo Fort to starboard as the river turns south towards Gillingham and the marshes give way to a built up area in the south. Then the river turns north past Chatham dockyard towards the steep wooded shore at Upnor. Masses of craft were racing but there was no problem avoiding them, for they were short tacking along the shore to dodge the tide while I went down the middle of the channel to get all the help I could from it. On past the training ship *Arethusa*, a four poster, once one of the famous German 'Flying P' class of square riggers in the South American nitrate trade. The river turns south again leaving Chatham on the east this time and Upnor Castle to starboard. The hills affect the wind here which came from the south-west both going and returning, although everywhere else it was south-east. Under Rochester Bridge at 1700 hrs with plenty of headroom although it was getting towards high water. Rochester Castle stands guard on the eastern shore but in complete contrast ahead is the spanking new M2 motorway bridge, giving fifty feet of headroom under its slim modernistic structure. A watery sun came out as I passed under and I enjoyed some pleasant sailing up the lovely Medway valley to reach Woodham at 1815 hrs by high water. Now I made a resolution many years ago never to dry out on the Medway between Allinton Lock and Rochester and this I kept, for at low water the river stinks. An hour later I was back through Rochester Bridge and wound my way past the *Arethusa* as they sounded eight bells. The sky was overcast now and a little light rain fell but I pressed on, for I wanted to make certain of leaving the river next morning if conditions warranted it. After overtaking a *Silhouette* I rounded up onto the mud at Bishops Oaze for the night and the other craft followed suit.

At 0500 hrs on Sunday, it was still overcast with a fine breeze from the south-west and I had visions of a record run to Suffolk. The tide was not high yet but this wind would carry me over the flood and I was soon underway. Coffee off Stansgate Creek at 0630 hrs as the wind died. I wrote in the log, 'What has Sheerness got against me that whenever I hove in sight they turn off the wind.' This has happened each visit for many years now. Out onto the Thames at 0715 hrs with the sun coming through the smoke haze. Some of the barges were motoring or being towed into the Medway, presumably for the race on Monday but a couple of traditionalists preferred to sail and gladden my eye that lovely morning. Up spinnaker and on sunhat (heat or sun stroke is one of my chief worries). Due to the calms we had experienced, the Thames was smooth as a mill pond and the Essex shore appeared as the sky cleared and the sun swallowed up the last vestiges of mist. Fourteen minutes to pass the measured mile off the edge of the Maplin Sands (alas no longer with us) with a little wind from the south-west but it died again and by ten o'clock I was drifting past the West Barrow in a dead calm. A wash and a shave in scorching sunshine. Wind from the south-east but it was too late for Suffolk now, so I decided to go round the Whittaker Beacon and run up the Crouch. It is a strange coincidence that I made the same passage in the same conditions last Whit Sunday (1964). At noon I found some seals on the sands and pulled up the plate to pass them as close as possible. Four of them leaped into the sea but 'grandfather' sat tight and even when I yelled at him, only moved halfway to the water. My how they glared at me! Now I know what those outboard motor types feel like when they belt through a fleet of sailing dinghies! One of the seals followed me for half a mile whilst the others soon nipped out onto the warm sand again. An increasing breeze from the south-east took me round the Whittaker at 1430 hrs and I got in the spinnaker for it was up to force four. A *Stella* was coming down from the Spitway but she never caught me until we reached the Roach at 1610 hrs, by which time the wind was easing again. At this time I had not realised the very poor performance of modern boats down wind unless they use a balloon spinnaker. At 1700 hrs I looked into Lion Creek and found plenty of water, after which I pushed on through Fambridge and into Stow Creek for a meal and a few minutes stretched out on the bunk, as the last of the flood trickled into the maze of creeks and flooded farmland on both sides of the river there. I left at 1910 hrs. As I reached the main stream, all the boats on the moorings were laying across the river, dead high water, but by the time I reached them they were streaming to the gathering ebb. With the wind in the south-east. *Shoal Waters* could nearly point down the river, in fact I only made eight tacks before mooring for the night about half a mile below the Roach at 2215 hrs.

Monday dawned overcast and misty but there were signs of blue sky higher up. The forecast was south-east one to three. It was dead calm as the last of the flood streamed into the river and I spent the time washing, feeding and getting things organised just that little bit better. One problem that I had never expected to befall me arose from half a dozen Christmas puddings that I had bought cheap a few days before the voyage began. Instead of the usual tins which stow well, these were pudding basin shaped on a flat square of cardboard covered in polythene and they would fit nowhere. Thus I found myself in the unhappy position of not knowing what to do with my Christmas puddings! Eventually I found room for them in my suitcase with books and papers. Cases were once taboo on small boats, but if there is a spare quarter birth they are ideal, provided they fit in.

As the tide turned at 0730 hrs I got under way with a little wind from the north-west. It soon went north, then north-east with a little rain. At Shore Ends at 0815 hrs the wind was south-east but not for long. The rain gave way to warm sunshine off the Sunken Buxey at 0915 hrs and by the time I reached the Ridge fifteen minutes later the wind had settled in the north-east. The meant a beat to Harwich. My standard plan in these circumstances is to stand out to sea and decide where to go when the tide turns. There was a lot of mist about and after passing the North Hook buoy, I was alone without a mark in sight. Port tack took me across the northern edge of the East Barrow Sand which was alive with indignant seals. We hear a lot about our crowded sailing waters but there is always plenty of space out here. After rounding the edge of the sands I stood on port tack until noon when a steamer passed ahead, then another. They must have been running up the Barrow deep from the light vessel which was honking somewhere out there in the mist. Visibility was at least half a mile most of the time and I was thankful for my tan sails which stand out so much better in a fog than white sails. Twenty minutes later I sighted Number Five Barrow to port and Number Six to starboard and tacked for the light vessel which appeared at 1300 hrs. The light appeared before the vessel itself which was just swinging to the new flood tide. The wind was more easterly and a little stronger. I rounded the light vessel at 1350 hrs and in view of the wind settling more easterly into a useful breeze, decided to press on for

Harwich over the flood tide. There is a cut across the Gunfleet Sand just north of the Old Light House so I steered 030 degrees to allow for the tide, guesswork rather than navigation. The following hour's sailing was the most pleasing of the day, with blue skies and warm sunshine on blue waves. The clouds rolled over again as I sighted the Gunfleet Lighthouse at 1445 hrs and sounded over the sands in four feet of water at 1600 hrs. A motor launch towing another loomed out of the mist from the Wallet side and headed for me. They were wearing the Cross of St George and must have been returning from the rally at Dunkirk to celebrate the evacuation twenty-five years earlier. As they drew near they must have spotted the Old Light House and steered away into deeper water. Today the old pile lighthouse makes one think of moon landing craft but things in space had not gone as far as that while I was on this cruise. A Gemini space craft was preparing to return to earth and they were speculating as to where she would land. I had my own problems. If I came out on the Naze it would mean a beat into Harwich. If I was too far east, I would waste time overshooting the entrance. At 1720 hrs the Medusa buoy came up bold on the port bow, just where I wanted it, and soon many boats appeared as the Naze itself loomed up, and later my old friend the Stonebanks buoy, a tubby little Pickwickian fellow with a red and white chequered waistcoat came into view. The wind was dying as I crept into Harwich at 1900 hrs on the last of the flood. As I reached the moored craft in the western part of the outer harbour the ebb set in, slowly at first, then fast and suddenly very fast indeed. I buoyed the anchor and dropped it over the side to avoid being swept back out to sea. This business of buoying the anchor is tricky when single-handed, and I worked out a scheme to have a line permanently tied to the crown of the anchor (which I carry with the arms vertical over the bows) with a line and buoy back in the cockpit. Then all I would have to do would be to throw the line and buoy overboard before going forward to let go the anchor. Getting under way, I would get the anchor normally and gather the line and buoy from the cockpit as the boat gathered way, provided that the line floated. Like so many bright schemes, I never persisted with it although it worked well enough. One reason was that I usually manage to moor in clear drying mud anyway and if I have to stay among moorings, the advent of these big plastic mooring buoys make it much easier to tie up to them than it was to pick up the older small buoys and heaving up fathoms of muddy rope to get at the chain. These days I carry a detachable boat hook which I use without the pole. After the line is made fast to the Samson post I can hook onto a buoy from the cockpit at leisure. The tide roared past me for the first hour causing the boat to sheer about alarmingly, through all of one hundred and twenty degrees, but it eased by the time I bedded down at 2100 hrs, without undressing in case the wind came up and made the place untenable. An hour later all was quiet, so I undressed properly and slept the sleep of the just as the rain began to tumble down.

When I woke at 0400 hrs it was still raining but there was a light breeze. This was no place to stay and I got away forty-five minutes later, feeling surprisingly cheerful in the circumstances; must be mad! The wind shifted north-east to north-west as I worked my way up the River Orwell on the last of the flood tide. To combat the rain I had a sunshine breakfast of cornflakes off Colimer Point and beat on past Pin Mill to Wolverstone where I got the 0640 hrs forecast of northerly winds about force three or four. At

0720 hrs I turned at Number Eight buoy and headed back down the river, for this seemed a good day for a grand run south through the Spitway to the Thames. Harwich breakwater abeam at 0930 hrs and over the ebb tide to the Naze to bring Walton pier in line at 1130 hrs. Rain, rain and more rain! For the first time, in my sailing career I did not care, for I had at last been able to afford a really good set of oilskins and never a drop came through. The pirate radio ships[3] floated by out in the east and I headed south, peering for the elusive Spitway buoy. It was moved about this time south-west, in fact we got the news in time for the Old Gaffers Race in July, but I shall never know if it was before or after this trip. Certainly it seemed to take a long, long time to appear but, of course, I was plugging the tide. My spirits were flagging a bit by the time it came up on the bow at 1300 hrs. As I rounded the spherical Wallet Spitway buoy the 1400 hrs forecast came over giving wind going lighter but staying north-west. It was just low tide and my spirits rose at the sight of three barges making down for the Spitway in time-honoured style. Two of them, *Millie* and *Venture* passed close enough to identify, but the other was too far away. A *Caprice* class cruiser was rounding the Whittaker having come from Burnham on the ebb. I expected to overtake her on this point of sailing but was almost dumbfounded just how quickly *Shoal Waters* swept past her. Admittedly she had a dinghy in tow and I did not, but the fact is that these small cruisers do not have enough sail once they come off the wind. If people will use these miserable little Bermudian mainsails like ocean racers, they

---

[3]*Caroline* (ex *Fredericksburg*) and *Atalanta* (ex *Mi Amigo*). Later they joined forces. Radio Caroline transferred to *Mi Amigo* and the original *Caroline* went to the Irish Sea.

must go the rest of the way and use big headsails and spinnakers. The north-east Maplin buoy passed to starboard at 1530 hrs as the last of the rain died away and then the Swin buoys began to roll by in fine style as the growing flood tide helped me on my way. Is there a better route to sail with a fair wind and tide anywhere in Britain?

The line of buoys and the sands on which they stand guard gradually curve westerly. Small craft can steer for the next buoy but one, thus cutting inside most of them, and sailing a shorter route *most* of the way. A trimaran appeared astern and seemed to be catching up fast. At this time multihulls were all the rage and expected to take over the whole sailing scene. I suspected that she was steering on me so that she cut even further inside the buoys. At 1705 hrs the Blacktail Spit buoy, a big black conical fellow, swept close by, swirling back and forth in the strong flood tide. It was now half flood and I was surprised to see dry sand inshore of the buoy. As I swung more westerly, the gleaming sand passed between *Shoal Waters* and the trimaran. This is one buoy you cannot cheat on. Suddenly the trimaran stopped, the sails fluttered and then came reluctantly down. It would be some time before she caught me up! The first of the measured mile beacons came in line at 1712 hrs and the others at 1724 hrs, giving me a speed over the ground of five knots in a light wind, with of course the aid of the fair tide.

The wind was more westerly now, the sea calm and the sky overcast with high cloud. I was not fussy where I ended up but preferred Leigh or Canvey as I had already been into the Medway. Thus I decided to head up past Southend Pier and keep the Medway in reserve in case the wind backed any more. The trimaran caught me up off the pier at 1835 hrs. I am no fan of multihulls but there is no doubt that these trimarans look at home in open water and far better than cats. As the wind died away I boiled a tinned steak and kidney pudding in the kettle and had supper as she glided the last mile to Leigh at 2000 hrs. They say one should pierce these tins first, but I have never had any trouble. I let the kettle boil and then turn out the gas and leave it for fifteen minutes to heat through. One of these days I shall forget the kettle and end up scraping the pudding off the deck-head!

Close to the jetty was a patch of open water. It seemed smooth enough to settle upon and I wondered why there were no boats moored there in such a convenient position. The sun, a dull red orb, appeared for a few moments before setting. The wind died completely, a few craft were trying an evening race but it was hopeless. Somehow I had got beyond the range of normal tiredness and had no inclination to crawl into the sleeping bag, so I busied myself fitting the new cockpit cover properly. Occasionally the boat rolled as wash from passing steamers out in the Thames moved slowly out towards the shore. The railway line is right on the coast here and I found myself blaming the wash on the trains. It goes to show the mistakes one can make when tired and the dangers of going on too long. I find that an initial tiredness gives way to seemingly limitless energy, and feel I could sail on for ever. No wonder people find themselves adding deviation instead of subtracting it! Navigators who won't sleep irritate me intensely offshore. On one Hook race our navigator mistook his landfall on the Dutch coast and sent us off down the coast with the tide under us and spinnaker set, when we should have beaten in the opposite direction. He could well have had twelve hours sleep on the broad reach from Smith's Knoll but he would stay on deck all the time.

Wednesday dawned dull and overcast with a forecast of winds from north-west force three or four. That soon settled my trip for the day, Sandwich; terra nova! I planned to walk ashore before the tide returned but soon realised why no boats moored in this area so close to the shore and the jetty. A deep creek, already full of water, ran between the boat and the shore. Anyway the tide soon came sweeping in over the flats and I sailed into the jetty under jib and tent, Norfolk Broads fashion. After posting the first of my films I did a little shopping, filled the water cans and took a load of gash ashore. The obvious place for the latter was a large litter bin but as I stuffed it in an old chap called out.

'Don't put it in there, leave it on the ground!' He assured me that he had to extract the contents of the bin through the same hole through which it was filled. By 0830 hrs all my business ashore was completed. I gave a local a lift out to his motorboat and set off eastward. In spite of the overcast sky, visibility was reasonable and I could see both shores clearly. In order to keep clear of the steamer lanes, I decided to cross to the Kent shore and take the Four Fathom and Gore channels to Margate, although I suspect that I lost some benefit from the ebb tide this way. The wind was dead astern so that the jib flapped idly but it was too rough to set the spinnaker. At 1000 hrs I was off the Nore Swatch and pleased to see a barge coming out of the Medway. She looked like the *Kitty* but she passed astern heading for the Swin. An hour later the Defence Boom off the Isle of Sheppey, a sort of king size garden fence built out across the shallow flats to keep out submarines in wartime, came in line. Although it was June, I was frankly cold and put on my oilskins for warmth. Further on at 'F'

Beacon I was pleased to see a strong ebb tide setting one hundred and twenty degrees, just the way I was going.

'At last I have caught them at it!' Just ahead of me in the haze, a vessel has the Spile buoy half out of the water. For many years, I and many other night class learn-it-by-the-book navigators have suspected that someone is going about the estuary swiping buoys and replacing them after we have passed by and crossed them off our charts. Now I have caught them in the act! They dropped it smartly into the water and made off into the mist when they saw me. 'They are only doing maintenance!' A likely story.

At noon I put up the spinnaker and *my!* how she drove along, but at Studhill an hour later I lost my nerve and got it down. By this time I had got in close to the Kent shore and my more easterly course kept the jib full, but she was much slower. A heavy rainstorm passed ahead over Margate while a line of white surf marked the edge of the Hook Sands, now dry for it was almost low water. At 1530 hrs I rounded the Longnose buoy and got that 'far away places', feeling for it is thirty miles from Southend and the south easternmost corner of the Thames Estuary. A swift tide was still going my way and would continue to do so for another three hours for the tide here runs out of step with the rest of the estuary. It also runs very hard, up to three knots. The gloomy white cliffs passed to windward as I turned south, and in the smooth water I brewed up and had a snack. By 1630 hrs I was off Ramsgate and hauling the sheets for a fine sail across the smooth shallow waters of Pegwell Bay. All signs of rain had gone by now and I picked out and sounded my way through a foot or two of water among the wide mud flats. The local seagulls were some of the fattest I have ever seen since my days with the Navy, and when a strong odour drew my attention to the rubbish dump over on the western shore, I realised why! The tide was already flooding and I was interested to see a fish trap on the mud. By 1730 hrs I was passing between steep muddy banks in a trickle of water.

At Richborough there is along well-made jetty but it seemed deserted except for one sand barge. This part of the trip is depressing at low water but it is a good chance to see obstacles near the banks and there are plenty of them. My Ordinance Survey map marks the Stonar Cut here, for the river almost turns back on itself after leaving the Old Cinque Port of Sandwich. It is a large weir, presumably used to let flood water get clear without passing through the town. The river grew more pleasant as Sandwich drew near. Trees appeared on the banks and a few inquisitive cattle gave me a look. At the town I moored in midstream below the ancient toll bridge and got the mast down, noting that the tide was flooding very strongly so it must have somewhere to go. A chap on a boat told me that there was another bridge just round the corner but that I should be able to get as far as Pluck's Gutter. It was just 1900 hrs. Most of the town is south of the river behind a high stone wharf. Beyond the bridge is a boatyard and derelict warehouses, but the river soon flows north again into open marshland with a power station dead ahead in the distance. I kept the mast down until I reached the second bridge but this was a mistake for it has long been removed. Only a better than average ability at map reading showed where it had been many years before. I rigged the mast and beat slowly towards the power station in the lightest of airs as darkness closed in. The Sonar cut from the up river side is rather like the head of water above a water mill and notices on the bank each side warn craft not to attempt to pass if the red flag is flying to show that the sluices are open. An estuary craft with an anchor has little to fear, but of course it could be dangerous for river craft with no ground tackle.

The power station was flooded with light at ground level and the tall cooling towers were marked with red lights, presumably to warn aircraft. Above them eerie clouds of hissing steam rolled out into the blue black sky. The river took me within yards of this hive of modern activity. Suddenly I sailed past into the cool night air among the marshes. One more bridge to duck under and I noted the wooden fender rails to protect the piers; a sure sign that boats once traded this way. There was a nice breeze by this time, as so often happens once night has fallen and although I had to beat, it was sheer pleasure all the way. I put the navigation lights on just to add glamour to the magic of the scene for there was little chance of meeting another craft. Herds of steers fattening on the marshes charged along the banks beside me and there was song in my heart. Suddenly they would pile up into a crush as they reached the dyke that served as the boundary of their domain. As I bid them goodnight another herd would come thundering out of the darkness to escort me for the next mile or two. By checking the bends of the river against the power station glaring astern, I was able to keep a check on my progress from the map. The iron bridge at Pluck's Gutter came into view at midnight. The moon was full. Every detail of the bridge was reflected in the still water to complete a scene of perfect peace that might well have been the Norfolk Broads. I dipped my hand in the water and tasted, as I expected, not a hint of salt!

Chapter Sixteen

Summer Cruise (Part Two)

Thursday dawned bright and clear with blue sky, warm sun, smooth water and every shade of greenery. The forecast was for wind from the north-west force four. It was a mistake not to have gone under the bridge last night while the tide was still flooding strongly, but of course I was tired and the rigging can get horribly tangled when lowering the mast in the dark. I washed and shaved, taking advantage of the fresh water on which she floated and enjoying sadistic thoughts on the discomfort of my barnacle passengers (fresh water kills them). By 0900 hrs the tide had still not begun to flood, so I got the mast down and walked her under the bridge. Of course I should have realised that the ebb here, so far from the sea, would be much longer than the flood, for the river has to carry a lot of water to the sea from the wide basin drained by the River Stour. This was sailing at its inland best. There are few trees, just an occasional stunted hawthorn and there was plenty of wind for the first few miles. The banks are lined with yellow irises in full bloom. By 1030 hrs I reached Grove Ferry, now a new bridge with a hotel and a cluster of houses with steeply rising ground on the north bank. Some two dozen craft were moored there, including the inevitable *Eventide*. The railway runs along the river edge here for a spell. A mile or so further on I was surprised to find a mine head and one of the conveyors went right across the river. Somehow Kent coal mines never seem to be so ugly as those in other parts of the world. Then the marshes on either side opened out into broad meres, too shallow to sail with the plate down but very easy on the eye (see fig. 9). The deep clear water became weedy, mostly lily pads as yet well below the surface. A smart motor runabout driven by an immaculately dressed young blade with the inevitable girlfriend in dark glasses passed me, the only other boat to do so all day.

'Have you really come all the way from Maldon in that?'

At noon I found a wire barrier right across the river supporting a structure to collect weeds cut further upstream. I grudged the time spent lowering the mast to pass under it and wondered if it was legal. The river was narrower now but still with room to tack with the plate half down and deep water right into the bank. I tried the old Norfolk Broads trick of grasping a handful of reeds to help her come round but they are not so sturdy here and broke off in my hand. Beyond the coal mine the river swung south-westerly and then north-west up to the last reach below Fordwich, which I have since learned, was the old port of Canterbury. At 1400 hrs I reached a bailey bridge half a mile below the town. The tide was beginning to ebb strongly and I decided that this was far enough. After mooring against the bank with the sails up to take some colour slides with the bridge and Fordwich church in the background, I set off for the sea. The wind had gone northerly and later north-east so that I had a lot of beating to do. Progress was slow but I was in no hurry in such a beautiful spot.

Above the coal mine I found my way out of the river and onto one of the broad meres but the water was less than two feet deep most of the way. Shale or waste from the pit seems to be used to preserve the actual banks of the river. My high-powered friend came along again with the offer of a tow, for which I thanked him but declined. Later on I found the launch moored against the bank, the occupants seemingly having vanished into some very thick scrub. Much later in the afternoon they caught me up again, looking a little less immaculate now, and offered to tow me again, obviously bewildered that anyone could bear to travel so slowly. At Grove Ferry the high bank carrying the railway line took most of the wind and the heat was stifling as I ducked the mast once more. By 1900 hrs I was back at Pluck's Gutter and found a better wind there, but now the ebb was nearly done. I towed from the bank for a time, glad of the first chance to stretch my legs since leaving Maldon, but was stopped by a wide dyke at 2100 hrs about half mile from the rail bridge. I decide to get some sleep while I had the chance.

Away again at 0200 hrs under a brilliantly clear moon in a flat calm I just drifted with the swift tide. Dawn came soon after I passed the power station and I reached Sandwich at 0700 hrs where I moored along the Hythe below the bridge. There were no steps and one has to climb the mast to get ashore at low tide. After an hour's sleep I went shopping and found it a delightful little town with a maze of streets. Luckily the boat was near the toll bridge, which is of course on the main road, for I would never have found it otherwise. I lost all sense of direction time and time again. Then back to the boat for a grand meal of thick steak, fresh rolls and fruit to finish, before getting some more sleep. The tide turned at 0900 hrs, but the water was rising fast an hour before this while the current still sluiced out to sea, a similar situation to that on the lower Bure on the Norfolk Broads. This whole area should be called the Kent Broads.

High tide was at noon. After a very thorough check of all the gear, I left at 1150 hrs as a light breeze filled in from the south-east. I was now at the south-east corner of the Thames Estuary so of course the wind went south-east! Once clear of the trees bordering the little town, I found good sailing all the way to the sea. Everything looked so much more attractive now that the water was level with the saltings. At 1315 hrs I was at the entrance and found the wind easing and seemingly going more southerly as I passed Ramsgate. I carried the spinnaker round to the North Foreland, debating along the way, the possibility of heading right across the estuary for Suffolk, but decided against it as I was short of sleep and might well get in a mess without the stamina to fight my way out of it. Round the Longnose buoy at 1445 hrs, a friendly little fellow warning vessels off a wide shelf of rock that juts out below the white chalk cliffs of the North Foreland. As the afternoon wore on I sailed steadily over the ebb tide past Margate to reach Herne Bay at 1830 hrs, about low water. Forty minutes later I crossed Whitstable Street in five feet of water on a lovely warm evening, with incredible visibility. The red sun was dropping into the water as I passed Harty Ferry at 2020 hrs. The plan had been to stop here and get down to some serious sleeping but there was a nice southerly breeze now and with a fair tide it seemed a pity to stop. The wind eased so I brought the cooker out into the cockpit and had another hunk of steak with fruit to follow. As I packed away the gear and drank my coffee, the wind increased a little as I met the flood coming in from the Medway at Elmley Ferry where the Swale turns northerly. The ships unloading and other harbour installations looked a pretty sight in the darkness under a full moon just ascending from the mass of buildings over Sittingbourne. Half an hour before midnight I anchored on the bend just below Ridham dock near a few moored yachts.

It was calm and overcast when I woke at 0500 hrs on Saturday morning. *Shoal Waters* was just afloat. The other craft on the moorings were already aground. Ugly lumps of clay torn from the saltings littered the mud, making it a very unpleasant place in which to dry out. I got away on the last of the ebb with a little breeze from the south-east. At low water I can pass under Kingsferry Bridge with the mast up, and this I did at 0620 hrs. The wind went south-west and increased as the ebb died and I had to beat into the River Medway over the first of the flood. As the Grain and Sheerness Forts came into view, I was delighted to see the barge *Memory* with her bowsprit down, setting off for Essex where she moors at Heybridge, a few hundred yards from *Shoal Waters*.

They would have a lot of tide to plug down the Swin, but they had a fair wind which increased as the morning wore on. I worked round the edge of the Grain Sand, keeping in the shallow water to dodge the flood tide while it was still going into the Medway. Once in the Thames, the tide was with me but I had to beat and for the first time this holiday it was almost reefing weather. Before getting out into the chop of the wide River Thames I hove to, a simple business of rolling up the jib and easing the mainsheet, in order to stow the gear properly, for I had not had time to do so when getting under way from Elmley that morning. At 1015 hrs I eased the sheets and turned north into Hole Haven, the creek between the western edge of

Canvey Island and the mainland. In bygone years it was the major yachting resort in Essex but now only the Lobster Pot Inn remains behind the sea wall as a relic of those days. Today oil and gas holders smother the marshes. Once into the Haven, the modern monstrosities dropped astern and I turned north-east along the creek to Canvey bridge at Benfleet as rain began to fall lightly. It was raining hard as I anchored near the bridge at 1130 hrs for a meal and a few minutes on my bunk to wait for high water for I had crossed the watershed behind the island and the flood tide was against me now.

As the flood died and the boat swung to the wind, the rain eased and I prepared to leave for Suffolk. I hadn't the heart to stop all that important road traffic so that they could open the bridge just for little me, so I ran up the mainsail and waited until another craft dropped her mooring and hooted for the bridge to open. Then I got the anchor and tacked under her stern to follow her through. They are certainly very quick on the bridge there for I was unable to see exactly to where the centre section vanished. I suppose that they got plenty of practice, for this bridge was the only road onto an increasingly prosperous and busy island.

I set the spinnaker as soon as there was room to let the boat look after herself for a spell, but the south-west wind died away and it was a long, long drift past the pier to the Defence Boom at 1515 hrs. Visibility was very poor on the Essex shore and for a time I was worried about the possibility of the tide carrying me towards the stakes of the boom, so that I would have to anchor and waste the rest of the tide. A little breeze came in at times and later on the visibility improved so that I could see right across the estuary to the twin towers at Reculvers on the Kent coast.

The measured mile took twenty minutes and by 1715 hrs I was off the Blacktail Spit. The wind continued to carry me over the tide slowly as the light faded. At the Maplin Spit at 1939 hrs I steered due north to take me out of the shipping lanes and over the shallow area known as Abraham's Bosom to anchor for the night at 2100 hrs. I slept like a log.

Sunday began with a light breeze from the west and a moon behind the clouds. The many buoys in the estuary did not show up at all well, but of course the Mid Barrow and Barrow Deep light vessels were unmistakable, for the powerful lights are forty feet above sea level which makes them visible for ten miles from a small boat. I left soon after midnight with the late, late show on the radio. It was impossible to pick out the Spitway buoys at first so I steered on the regular white flash of the Barrow Deep light vessel, knowing that any lights that appeared on the port hand must be the Spitway, which I found and passed through at 0200 hrs. In light airs I continued down the Wallet as the lights on the Essex shore appeared one by one. A solitary coaster came past me bound for the River Colne, the only company I had all night. It began to rain lightly, but I was so warm and cosy in my duffel coat that I kept it on instead of my oilskins. It meant a wet duffel coat which can be a dead loss on a small boat unless the next day is hot enough to dry it out. With this poor progress, it was out of the question to get into the River Ore soon after low water, although a light westerly wind is ideal for crossing the dangerous, ever-shifting shingle bar. It was important for me to carry the flood tide right up to the first road bridge fifteen miles up the river at Snape on the midday tide and I did not want to spend two precious days in one river while the good weather lasted. Thus I decided to go into Walton Backwaters on the midday tide and then enter the Ore in the evening on the first of the flood, to visit Snape on Monday. I passed Walton Pier at 0420 hrs and worked round the back of the Naze, swinging the sounding pole like a walking stick to find the entrance to the gut where I anchored in six feet of water at 0530 hrs. It was important that I didn't ground, for there is a lot of rock about here. The Gut is a short cut inside the notorious Pye Sand which stretches from Walton Stone on the western side of the entrance, halfway to Harwich Breakwater. It dries completely at low water but soon fills once the flood starts, leaving dry sand at high Hill for another couple of hours. Shallow craft can use it from about half flood instead of going right out to the Pye End buoy. I woke to find the rain gone and a warm sun drying out the boat again. After a lazy breakfast and a good wash and shave, I left at 0915 hrs with a useful breeze from the south-west and found three or four feet of water all the way to the main channel. Under a brilliant June sun I beat down Hamford Water and south between Horsey and Skippers island. This must be some of the most pleasant sailing to be found on the East Coast! I wound my way into Kirby Creek and worked across the Wade, the shallow area south of Horsey Island. The watershed is the mile long hard causeway over which all traffic to and from the island must pass. There was just enough water for me to cross, but of course it is the watershed and I found a strong tide against me along the Twizzle until I got back into Walton Creek where the flood helped me up to the Walton and Frinton YC at 1145 hrs. Walton is a pleasant spot. It is only a few steps from the club and public hard to the shops and the sea front. It took me just thirty minutes to fill the water cans from the hose at the jetty, phone my wife, do some shipping, buy fish and chips and leave with a rising wind on the first of the ebb at 1215 hrs.

Half an hour or so later I anchored on the western edge of the entrance and settled back to watch the fine craft entering and leaving in the strong breeze which was now gusting five or six at times. I take it that there is a weekly pilgrimage of Walton yachts to Pin Mill and a similar one from Pin mill to Walton, which adds up to a colourful picture as they make their way home on a fine Sunday afternoon. It was also a good chance to air my bedding, for things had got a little clammy although no actual water had got to them.

The next problem was to decide the time to leave for the River Ore. It is no use arriving too soon, for the ebb tide runs out very strongly, making it nearly impossible to enter until slack water. Waiting about outside for the tide to turn in the river can be a tedious business as there is a rare old popple where the ebb running north-east up the coast collides with the ebb coming south-east out of the river. Low water was at 1830 hrs and I had to be well on the way by this time, in case the wind died and I was unable to carry on up the coast over the flood tide coming south. I left at 1445 hrs under full sail, wondering if I ought to have reefed. Ten minutes later I was hardly moving through water in almost flat calm. So it continued throughout the afternoon. Dark squally clouds would bring strong winds and then move off to leave smooth water and a scorching sun.

This time I took the proper channel out of Walton Backwaters along the line of buoys laid by the Walton and Frinton YC black to port and red to starboard (for I was leaving harbour now and thus reversed the handing of the buoys). Each is based on a wooden beer barrel. They seem to have a good supply of empties! Some are numbered, others are named, such as High Hill, marking the first of the sand to appear as the tide drops, Crab Knoll where the channel narrows and then Pye End with its cage top-mark. The usual procession of steamers was leaving and arriving at the thriving port of Harwich. I worked my way across to the Cork light vessel at 1615 hrs and ran in towards Bawdsey Haven to get some slides of the approaches. Then I bore away again towards the Ore which I reached at exactly 1800 hrs, but the ebb in the river had another hour to turn. There were several larger craft outside waiting to get in. The shingle bank to the north of the entrance was the largest that I have ever seen, but no shingle showed above the water south of the swirl of smooth water pouring out of the river. It was out of the question to beat in over that tide so I decided to try my luck over the south bar. Experience has taught me that there is often more water close to the shore than out towards the entrance buoy. I stood in and went over in three feet of water. Once into deep water, I came hard on the westerly wind, port tack, but it was no use as I just crabbed across to the north bank, losing ground all the way. Then I noticed a tiny bay at the edge of the shingle. A few moments later *Shoal Waters'* bow slid into the shingle and I jumped ashore with the anchor. Spurred by my example, an *Atalanta* came in under motor but found it a long slow job. This was my first chance to walk over these banks. There were several other channels out to the north but they only had a trickle of water in them. An old chap fishing from the shingle forecast that the entrance was due for a big change and a year later I found a much more regular and simple entrance. The *Atalanta* made sail as soon as she got round the corner. By looking every five minutes it was just possible to see that she was moving up river.

Back aboard the boat, I brewed tea and did a few odd jobs as the ebb slackened. One by one the other craft came in under roaring motors. Little wavelets appeared on the water where previously wind and tide together had left a smooth surface. It was time to go. At 1900 hrs I entered the river and sailed slowly up to Orford as the wind died. A Christmas pudding simmered in the kettle as I passed the bird sanctuary of Halvergate Island and when the wind failed I anchored under the north shore below Orford for a well-earned, full night's sleep.

Monday dawned fine and warm with light wind from the north-east but as the day wore on it went right round through east, south to south-west by nightfall. I left at 0730 hrs. The little port of Orford sheltering beneath its ancient castle keep, looked like something out of a travel brochure. On the mud I spotted *Willy Nilly*, a traditionally built Yorkshire cobble made famous by the writer John Seymour who sailed her down the coast and later across to Denmark. It is worth noting that sailing craft died out on other parts of the coast far earlier than in the Thames Estuary. He was unable to find many people alive who had sailed these cobbles with their lug rig, which was soon forsaken once the infernal combustion engine made an appearance. I suspect this is due to two factors, firstly that the craft themselves never reached the perfection of the Thames craft and that the areas in which they were used favoured sail less than the Thames, with its clockwork tidal currents which can be used to offset foul winds. I saw five laden barges under sail come into Stone Heaps at Shotley as late as 1949. Certainly John Seymour spent a lot of time being towed and later used a motor on his cobble. The commercial sailing craft have gone from the Thames today, but those factors which kept them alive so long still make this the perfect area for small yacht cruising.

In fact Orford belied its ancient appearance. There was a top secret defence establishment on the shingle opposite the town and large numbers of workers were ferried across by tank landing craft each morning to work there. After my Royal Marine days, these craft fascinated me. The wind was light but the tide flowed strongly. After Orford the river becomes the Alde and flows parallel to the shore for another five miles to Slaughden, where only a stone jetty marks the village that once had twenty-seven children in its school. I nosed *Shoal Waters* into the smooth mud and clambered ashore to plant the anchor in the saltings which were smothered in tiny sea pinks. Then armed with camera and binoculars I walked across the narrow salting, up the bank and looked out to the open sea, only a few yards or so from *Shoal Waters*. It was still possible to climb into and to the top of the Martello tower although it becomes more vandalised each season. From the top I got some fine slides of the little town of Aldeburgh and the narrow isthmus between the river and the sea. Millions of pounds have been spent to keep the sea and river apart here for once they joined, Father Neptune would give the town short shift. The sea front Guild Hall at Aldeburgh was built in Elizabethan times three streets back from the waterfront. Memories of the erosion of Dunwich, a few miles away to the north, still live on here. Now they have a light railway carrying shingle from the south, where the shingle spit is half a mile wide, to build up the sea defences here. It bewilders me that no attempt is made to keep the Martello tower in good preservation. Built to oppose Napoleon, used for observation in the Kaiser's and again in Hitler's war, straddling this most desperate long drawn out battle against coast erosion, surely we cannot just let it fall down![4]

The wind was easterly now and I got back to the boat for the journey to Snape, the maltings by the first road bridge. The fine house in Blackheath Woods was a breathtakingly beautiful sight, the orange red brickwork standing out against the deep green of the pine trees, above a bank of purple rhododendrons on top of a low sandy cliff at the water's edge. It cannot be viewed from the road but this time I got some good shots with my camera. On through Iken and up the last winding mile to Snape at 1215 hrs. This was rural Suffolk at its best. A meal and a snooze as the last of the flood made. How I sympathise with those chaps who sail about with a private lead mine slung several feet under their craft and cannot reach places such as this; almost as much as they sympathise with me out at sea when they slam past to windward, leaving me bobbing about like so much flotsam. In my view the deep keel man on this coast is like a blind man having a day out in a nudist camp; he can enjoy the sunshine and fresh air, but is unable to appreciate other interesting aspects of the situation.

There wasn't much flood left at 1400 hrs so I got underway and beat down the river into the breeze from the south-east. The bends of the river seemed to fit the tacks and I made fine progress to Iken at 1445 hrs after which the wind was free for a couple of miles. At Slaughden there was enough south in the wind to make it a beat to the entrance. Here the drying mud was actually steaming in the searing heat as it uncovered. At Orford at 1645 hrs the wind was south south-west force three. Below Halvergate Island, where the two halves of the river rejoin, an object on the far

---

[4]The Martello tower has now been restored as a private residence.

shore to which the starboard tack was carrying me, caught my attention. I swung up my glasses and found it to be real blonde Venus type creature standing stretching out in the sunshine. While trying to decide if she was wearing a pink bikini or if the lighter patches were her genuine not quite so sunburnt self, I noticed a great big hairy six-foot-two sitting beside her watching me through a powerful pair of glasses, whereupon I discontinued my enquiries and made that tack a short one.

It was just 1800 hrs as I reached the bar and had a smooth passage out. An eighteen foot Blackwater sloop was making her way in slowly over tide with, of course, a fair wind today. Over the next half an hour I watched her creep round the bend, almost inches at time. Once over the south bar, I tacked inshore where there must be some sort of an eddy, for the tide was already going my way. The lobster pots marked by long lines of corks with a float of some sort and often a flag at the very end are a useful guide to the set of the tide. In the post-war years there were many of them about; then the trade seemed to slacken off. As I write, things have bucked up again with the rising price of lobsters. Of course it does not do to get tangled with them, particularly with an engine going. That lot round the prop soon makes an auxiliary craft a pure sailorman and the motor craft into a salvage job.

By the time I reached the Deben at Bawdsey Haven, the waves were getting larger and the sun had an unfriendly glint about it which was reflected in a hard sheen on the water. It looked as though the fine spell was about to end. I always find the entrance to the Deben far more difficult than the Ore. There are leading marks but it is a job to know when to line them up and I was glad to follow a motor craft in, finding four feet all the way. In view of the possible change in the weather and the fact that I had explored the river right up to the Wilford Bridge at Easter, I decided to take the night flood to the town and come back at once to get into the Harwich complex of rivers, which is a far more interesting place in which to be weather-bound. Ramsholt at 2030 hrs and on past Waldringfield forty-five minutes later where I met Ronald Simper in *Sea Fever,* one of our Old Gaffers Association craft, who waived to me cheerily. Meeting friends such as this means a lot to the single-handed even if it is only a passing wave. In the wooded banks below Waldringfield, I noticed an *Enterprise* at anchor and up among trees a steep path led to a bright orange tent, alongside which a couple were sitting admiring the sunset, a most happy picture. At dusk I moored inside the lines of craft opposite the Woodbridge YC and so to sleep.

It was overcast when I left on Tuesday with wind from the south, force two. I made steady progress through Ramsholt at 0500 hrs and over the bar fifty minutes later. By this time it was getting lively with the wind SE force four. I carried full sail in order to have plenty of steerage way across the difficult entrance which is partly sheltered by the high shingle banks, but once outside I soon pulled down a reef, the first of the holiday. The forecast at 0640 hrs gave south-west five to six and later in the day a gale warning came through. It was with real relief that I eased the sheets round the Beach End buoy to race into Harwich before the rising sou'wester, as sailing craft have done over the centuries. Next I disgraced myself by keeping too close to the Harwich town shore and ran aground on the spit that runs out beyond the moored craft towards the Guard buoy. Of course this was the first time that I had entered Harwich so early on the tide. Round into the Stour at 0800 hrs for a fine sail to Wrabness for breakfast in warm sunshine as *Housewives Choice* came over radio. The long calm weather had allowed the water to become very clear and when I anchored near the ridge of clay that gives a cliff of sorts at Wrabness five miles up river from Harwich, I was surprised to see the anchor hit the bottom ten or twelve feet down.

Breakfast and a wash in leisurely time for there was no hurry. The Stour is very shallow and normally the intending explorer need not leave Harwich until two hours after low water. The channel from here is marked for the benefit of barges to the maltings and seed mills at Mistley where there must be over a thousand swans. Many were moving downstream and I noted that they were smart enough to keep in shallow water out of the strong flood time, and some even preferred to walk along the edge of the mud flats. At Manningtree, only the channel itself had any water, but I just managed to reach the end of the hard at 1045 hrs for a quick shopping expedition. More fresh steak. Last year I ducked under the bridge on the southern of the two creeks above the village. This time I went north, close reefed now, and ducked under rail bridge and then the famous Cattawade bridge, noting the wooden rails protecting the piers supporting the middle arch, a sure sign that boats traded here in days gone by. With the wind and tide behind me, it was easy progress with the mast down, but coming back would be a different problem. In fact I found little above the bridge. The old mill race was being used as a rubbish dump and the mill is derelict. I penetrated past a dam, which I presumed was once the entrance to the canal to Flatford Mill of Constable fame and wound my way into a mass of reeds, taking the widest channel at each junction until the waterway was narrower than my boat was long. Eventually I came alongside a reed-bank separating the channel from the canal. It looked as though I could get across at high spring tides but this was not the time for such tricks. (In 1969 I found that the dam was the lock gates and *Shoal Waters* became the first sailing craft to get from the sea to the mill for many years). It seemed a strange set up, for I had found what seemed to be the remains of a sort of lock gates on the southern arm (later information suggests that this may have been the remains of a wooden footbridge). As most of the journey since the bridge had been to windward it was an easy run back once I had turned the boat round. This proved a major problem. I pulled the stern into a side creek but as the head turned homewards, the wind filled the mainsail and drove her into the bank again before there was time for the rudder to take control. Anyway, she made it at the forth or fifth attempt at the cost of a very muddy stem and bowsprit. Actually it was an advantage that the tide was still flooding at Cattawade bridge, as wind and tide held the boat away from the bridge while I lowered the mast. Then I worked her under, handling her along the woodwork, and a final push carried me a few dozen yards downstream to anchor while I rigged the mast. It was a nuisance, but it seemed to be the only way to reach the rail bridge two hundred yards downstream. After a couple of tacks I realised that the power lines across the river were too low for me to sail under. Down mast again and this time I towed from the bank and fortunately the old wooden walk under the rail-bridge was still in place. The timber was too broken to lie against as I rigged the mast, so I pushed out to anchor again.

It was hard sailing until I reached Manningtree, from where it was a fair wind all the way to the obvious place to shelter, Pin Mill. Progress eased a little in the shelter of

Mistley with its tall buildings perched on the very edge of the river at the bottom of the cliffs, but soon speeded up again as the southern shore dropped back from the river. It was a wild sight off Harwich at 1555 hrs and I came on the wind and tacked, rather than risk a gybe in that lop. Progress was slower over the ebb in the River Orwell, but eventually I rounded Colimer Point and in fact had to shake out the reef once in the shelter of the trees below Pin Mill. At 1700 hrs I ran onto the mud near the hard, welcomed by a *Spitfire* class cruiser, *Tina*, who I had met at Great Wakering last Easter. A walk ashore to post a letter and get some water. Then to sleep and sleep and sleep. I needed rest. It had seemed criminal to stop while wind and tides served, but now I knew just what to do. Head down at 2130 hrs and there I stayed until 0830 hrs on Wednesday.

The gale warning was still in force next morning so I decided to stay put for the day. Peter rowed over from *Tina* while his breakfast was cooked for him and we decided to meet ashore for a yarn that evening. It was far too muddy where I lay and not particularly well sheltered at the top of the tide, so I decided to move over against the western shore where there is only a few inches of mud over firm clay. I examined it carefully with my glasses while the tide was out, for there is all manner of junk about there from old anchors to large rocks. At 1100 hrs when she floated, I sailed over for a better look and then sailed around for an hour until the tide reached the spot where I wished to moor. At noon I beached and walked over the berth, removing a few hazards and putting out a stern line to an old deeply embedded anchor. I would of course use my own anchor forward. Once moored, I walked ashore and had a stroll until the tide left her at about 1500 hrs. Thus passed a pleasant day with a little rain in the evening, by which time I was high and dry in the Butt and Oyster pub.

I had no desire to spend another day high and dry so listened to the 0200 hrs forecast, ready to move out into deep water or even sail right away. It was force nine. I stayed and slept on! The wind veered north-west during the night and even keel boats on the moorings had a very rough time. *Shoal Waters* lay steady as a rock on the sand while the wind screamed through the tops of the trees ashore. Next morning the rain had gone but the wind was still strong. In the calm where I lay on the mud it was stifling hot, and I sweated as I did a couple of hours hard labour clearing some the odds and ends off the mud to make it a better, safer place for boats to lay. Next time I come this way I may not have so much time to choose a berth. The wind eased as the tide ran back in and I got away up river to Ipswich in the afternoon, shaking out the reefs for the run back downstream with the ebb. The 1800 hrs forecast came over as I was beating out across Dovercourt Bay, giving south-west force six, which killed any chance of a night passage round the coast, so I turned across the Pye Sand and found four feet near Crab Knoll to get into the Walton Channel. The wind began to pipe up again so I anchored to reef down before beating into the Backwaters where I found the best shelter I could near Foundry Hard at 2030 hrs.

Friday's forecast was south-west force six, seven or eight. My plans to visit the Medway again and finish off the holiday with a Saturday afternoon passage through Havengore were now out of the question. It would be a struggle to get home. Walton is not the best place to lay ready for a run south so I decided to go back to Shotley, the traditional place to lay waiting for a favourable wind shift. It was a lively trip, taking one and a half hours to arrive off Stone Heaps at 1230 hrs. The rest of the day passed quietly, getting plenty of rest and packing the gear better than before. The remaining tea bags were repacked into a smaller packet so that they didn't rattle so much when I came about! The evening forecast began to talk of the wind moderating tomorrow, but gale force warnings were still in force. After the tide had half gone, I moved the boat up to the mud and had a walk ashore. The method in these circumstances is to let her drop back on a long chain, then pull up to the anchor, snatching it out of the mud as she passes over it. Then she will carry her way many yards, but once she stops I drop the anchor and repeat the performance. It was a very clear evening as the sun went down and the Felixstowe shore stood out very vividly indeed. I bedded down, confident of better things on the morrow.

The 0200 hrs forecast still gave the gale warning but things seemed quieter. I sailed out of the harbour but there was nothing to be gained so I ran back to Shotley for another sleep in the first light of dawn. The morning forecast gave west four to six, going south-west three to five. Away in fighting trim and wearing a safety harness for the first time this trip at 0700 hrs. Half an hour later I cleared the harbour to find a lovely boisterous sea that showered me with sparkling spray. Gone was the murderous vicious intent of yesterday. The sky seemed bluer, the shores greener than I can ever remember them before. If only I could have kept the camera going, but it is not waterproof, and in any case I had my hands full sailing the boat. Once I reached across Dovercourt Bay to the shelter of the Naze, things got quieter and I had a brew up. At Walton Pier at 0915 hrs I came hard on the wind on starboard tack which carried me almost to the Spitway. By this time the wind was easier and I took a few slides, including an ocean racer that romped past me. Closer inshore, I put up the big jib and rounded Colne Point at 1320 hrs. There were three barges off Mersea Stone, *Memory*, *Kitty* and could it be? Yes it was. The *Mirosa* out on her first trip after a year's refit in the canal at Heybridge. It was the first time I had seen her owner, Claud Duval, relaxing since he bought her. He certainly looked a most happy fellow sitting in the sunshine out of the wind. Long may people toil to keep barges sailing on the East Coast.

I beat up to Colchester (for there was some north in the wind now) reaching the Hythe at 1625 hrs. A coaster, *David,* came up with me on the tide, loaded cattle from waiting lorries and then left again at once. On the way down the river, I called into Thorrington Creek, for the swinging rail bridge over the river is now permanently open. It is a lovely spot but should only be visited on a rising tide as there is far more mud than water. Back past Mersea Stone and into Ray Creek behind St Osyth for the night. I beached on mud with the bow over the shingle bank so that I could walk along the shore as the sun set over Mersea. It always pays to watch points like this and my efforts were well rewarded. The creek was alive with fish by low water.

On Sunday, a bright sunrise over the Martello tower on the grassy cliff brought another perfect day but this time with westerly winds of force two or three. I left at 0545 hrs and ran out to the Buxey Beacon at 0745 hrs, returning northwards until the power station was in line with St Peter's on the Wall, which put me north of Batchelors Spit.

I anchored for breakfast and a wash and to wait for the flood tide into the river. What a difference from yesterday!

The wind piped up to a fine working breeze on the way to Maldon at 1600 hrs from where I ran back to my mooring to end a perfect holiday cruise. The distance covered was some 588 nautical miles in one hundred and ninety hours sailing. The average of just three knots was low but then the winds had been very light. There had been no heroics, I never got soaked to the skin, the jam never got mixed up with the tinned milk and nothing carried away. *Shoal Waters* may not be everyone's ideal boat, but this cruise proved how suitable she is for this region, with its rich variety of rivers and shallow offshore banks.

Chapter Seventeen

Two Weekends in April

Not a drop of wind. Water like a mirror under a full moon. A bite in the air that reminded me that Easter sailing is usually a cold game and certainly likely to be so this year with the forecast from the weather centre at Mildenhall suggesting north-east winds around force four or five over the holiday. *Shoal Waters* was already afloat but there was no question of setting off down river without wind for the tide would flood for another three hours yet. I left Roy to carry on sleeping and set about one of the essential sailing tasks that I really loathe, washing the wellington boots in which we had walked out to the boat through the mud just before dark. It's a job that cannot be done until the tide returns but of course we had tied them to the boat so that they couldn't float away. The job completed, I dived back into the tiny cabin until high tide.

By 0010 hrs on Good Friday when we slipped from the mooring a nice breeze had filled in from the north-west. High water was at 0035 hrs so that by the time we passed Osea Pier at 0050 hrs the ebb was helping us on our way and the wind was already veering. This was the first trip that Roy, who had recently bought a clinker built sixteen footer with a tiny cabin, called a *Wright Weekender*, had made with me since 1954. He wanted some 'real' cruising but had to be back home by Sunday evening and had left his car at Chelmsford. I assured him that my aim was to get in plenty of sailing and, if possible, visit Kent and Suffolk over the four days of Easter, an aim which continues to elude me. My new paraffin navigation lights burned brightly as did the little paraffin lamp in my fine brass compass. (I have long since recognised that electricity is here to stay and now carry a twelve volt battery which is charged up at home).

Roy ducked back into his bunk out of the cold to get some rest, for we had agreed that he would take over at dawn. Several other craft left Maldon with us but all except one anchored off Osea Island in the traditional anchorage east of the pier. I stayed close hauled on port tack which took us over Thirslet Spit, but of course with a centreboard I have no worries and expected the wind to continue to veer. By the time we reached the Spitway at 0330 hrs it had gone round to north-east but we got out of the river without putting in a tack. A bold green light showed clearly over the far side of the Swin and I was excited to realise that it was a sailing barge under way, the first I had ever encountered at night. As we gradually overhauled her and passed under her stern I was able to read her name *Centaur*. In brilliant moonlight, with the Whittaker Beacon silhouetted in the track of the moon, she was a breathtakingly beautiful sight. One chap was at the wheel and another at his side. The whole wood and canvas monster was as steady as a rock while we dipped and rolled violently. Once the flood set in, the buoys along the edge of the fifteen mile long Foulness Sands slipped by rapidly as dawn reluctantly revealed itself on the port quarter. Roy took over at the Maplin Spit buoy at 0545 hrs. The wind was almost dead astern and he called me to take in a reef off the West Oaze at 0750 hrs. The sun had appeared now and Roy needed the warmth, for he hadn't taken my warning to bring plenty of warm clothing seriously enough.

At 0905 hrs we passed between the Medway Forts at Sheerness and were glad to find smoother water, for things outside were getting very lively indeed. It was three years since I had been under Rochester bridge and twenty since I had reached Aylesford. With a fair wind and fair tide, there was only one logical route. Through Rochester at 1130 hrs after a quick look into the Hoo Marina to find some friends, and on under the new M2 motorway bridge which provides such a vivid Contrast with the ancient stone bridge at Aylesford which we reached at 1345 hrs. Over fifty-six miles in thirteen hours thirty-five minutes; an average speed of just over four knots. One lives in hope of a one hundred and eighty degrees wind shift on these occasions but none was coming and it would be a long hard trip home. But at least we had plenty of time in hand. We spent over an hour there, dining on thick steak fried in butter with plenty of strong tea. It's an enchanted spot. I was fascinated by the buttresses at the sides where pedestrians could step out of the way of the horse drawn traffic. Today the bridge only takes eastbound vehicles and a bailey bridge, mercifully out of sight upstream, deals with westbound traffic. As we set out on the long beat back down river, the sun vanished behind the clouds that had been gradually filling the sky and it was a long cold trip to Chatham where we moored for the night. I was in my bunk by the 1800 hrs forecast which gave north to north-east four as a few spots of rain splattered.

Low water Sheerness on Easter Saturday was 0747 hrs. If we were to beat the rest of the way down the Medway to get into the West Swale before the tide turned we should have to leave at 0500 hrs but it was so nice in the old sleeping bag and the light rain outside sounded so unpleasant that I was an hour late. The wind was light at first but came in with the flood tide and we had a hard beat down river. I had decided that if we couldn't reach the Swale by 1000 hrs we would drop back and explore Stansgate Creek but we just made it. It was time for a reef now. We tore past Queenborough and up to Kingsferry bridge with just enough headroom to sail under. At Elmley Island we anchored for a meal and then beat eastward making slow progress, as the tide was now flooding from the east against us until high water. Close reefed by this time, we realised that it would be out of the question to take the ebb across the Thames. (We learned later that two or three people were drowned that day a few miles behind us.)

'I'll take you into one of the loneliest parts of England,' I promised Roy.

'Windmill Creek winds into the island for four miles and from the head of the creek we can walk to the north shore and watch the sun go down from the cliff top.' Alas it was a long time since I had come this way and was disappointed to find the creek damned off. We made the best of it by beaching just west of Harty Island and spent a warm and pleasant afternoon walking over the low hill. We returned to the hill top to watch the sunset and then dived back into those lovely warm bunks. This time it was Roy's turn to wash the water-boots when she floated at 0130 hrs. It was a lot calmer but I decided to wait for the forecast before sailing.

The 0200 hrs forecast gave NE 4/5/6.

'Right! Time to go!' It was a wonderful night and with the high tide we could see right across the Isle of Sheppey from east to west behind Elmley and Harty islands. Roy seemed in two minds at first. It was warmer in the cabin but sea sickness is inevitable and I suggested he wrap up well and sit out in the cockpit for this would be a sail to remember. It was a long beat before we could point north past the island but then we spotted the lights marking the Red Sand Tower and this made a good mark to steer on. It was just getting light as we passed the deserted gun tower. The moon was clear in the sky and a small coaster passed behind us. Apart from that we were alone with the waves. Roy had heard so much about crowded sailing waters around our shores and marvelled at our wide open playground. In fact I allowed a little too much for the tide and we got right over onto the Essex shore by the Maplin buoy, making extra windward work down the Swin. Here the seas were frighteningly high and it became plain that we would be nowhere near the Whittaker Beacon by low water. At 0930 hrs I eased over onto Foulness Sands into smooth water sheltered by dry sand to the north-east and we had a quick brew up. The beacon bore 050m, the SW Middle 113m and there seemed to be water all the way bearing 320m. The sands were covering rapidly and we moved in a little further after about fifteen minutes. This time we could see the Ridge buoy bearing 343m. Whittaker Beacon 069m and SW Middle 120m. The barge *Kitty* coming down the Whittaker Channel encouraged us to get underway again and this time we got right across to the tail of the Buxey. *Kitty* sailed round the barge *Marjorie* who was at anchor in the Rays'n. 'Coming out to play,' one could almost imagine her asking. She did just that and the two of them romped off towards the Swin like a couple of young puppies. From now on with a flood tide and rising north-east wind it was all plain sailing. Roy packed his gear and I dropped him off on Burnham town steps at 1215 hrs. He stepped almost straight onto a bus and picked up his car at Chelmsford. I pressed on with the tide, behind Bridgemarsh Island and moored in Stow Maries Creek for a meal and a nap at 1330 hrs.

I had visions of a record trip down the river with the spring ebb tide but the wind was almost gale force at HW and I decided on a little more sleep, leaving at 1730 hrs by which time things were much quieter and moored at Key Reach 2015 hrs.

Monday morning high water was 0240 hrs. The water was smooth and the wind light with a grey mantle of cloud overhead. I left at 0500 hrs and beat out to sea. By 0700 hrs I was off the Whittaker Beacon with plenty of time in hand and decided to have a look at the East Barrow Sand where I cornered a seal and managed to get a close up colour slide which has delighted audiences ever since. What a contrast from yesterday! I was able to run the boat up the beach onto a dead lee shore so smooth was the sea. Then I set off for home with the flood tide, drifting hove too off West Mersea while I washed and shaved before disgracing myself by walking into a chandlers for a pair of sailing shoes and coming out with a smart new copper anchor light. No doubt about it, the only way to avoid spending money is to keep sailing! Off the western end of Osea Island I anchored for my last meal of the voyage before picking up my mooring. This turned out to be the most dangerous part of the trip when I became the turning mark for water skiers. One passed me eight times in thirty minutes, often within a few yards. At 1500 hrs I picked up my mooring after a trip of one hundred and seventy-five miles in eighty-seven hours. I often feel a tinge of conscience about my crew members but they always come back. That evening I got a call from Tony, one of last years victims and he booked up for the following weekend.

Tony's trip a week later was a complete contrast. High water was at 1715 hrs on Friday night and we left at 1830 hrs with a forecast of southerly 4/5 all over the weekend. I slept a little as Tony steered down river. Bradwell Power station was abeam at 2045 hrs and the wind eased as we rounded the Denghie Flats. Just for the hell of it we found the unlit Buxey Beacon in the dark for the moon was late rising. It came out of the night just where we expected from bearings taken on the Wallet Spitway light buoy and the Sunken Buxey. Tony bedded down as we reached the deep water of the outer Crouch at 0045 hrs and I pressed on to Havengore at 0400 hrs where I anchored and got my head down. The voice of the bridge keeper woke us at 0600 hrs and ten minutes later we were on our way towards the Thames. The wind was SE 2 and once out of the creek, Tony steered south on port tack while I slept. When I looked out again Sea Reach No 1 was to starboard and a warm sun was killing off the faint breeze. We carried on slowly, being swept eastwards by the tide more than we were moving south under sail. At 0945 hrs we kedged off the West Middle. Zephyrs came and went as we worked slowly towards the shore and I eventually polled her round the Ham Gat at 1330 hrs and left Tony to sail westward with a breeze from north-east about force 2 while I slept again. There had been a forecast of SW4 but we never saw any sign of it. It was a delightful trip but there was not enough room under Kingsferry Bridge. We hoisted a bucket and sailed back and forth but got no acknowledgement from the bridge keeper. A train had passed over as we approached and we did not expect there would be another. After about fifteen minutes we decided they were not going to open up and made over to the north shore and got the sails down. I was just about to lower the mast as a train rattled over. That was why they had not opened up! We made sail again as the bridge rose sharply but the wind was lightish and we made slow time of it. I kept the camera going and was told by an irate bridge keeper.

'Put that bloody camera away and come under the bridge.' The tide floods eastwards here and it took some time to get through. I trembled to think what he would have said if by the time he opened up, we had got the mast down and pushed under! We would have done this near the shore so he would have had no way of knowing where we were!

The wind lasted to get us over the flood to Sheerness but once there we drifted while waiting for the ebb and eventually beat out across the Thames as the sun went down. This was against all my principles of never being in the open Thames after dark but we had to get home. At 2100 hrs we crossed the Yantlet dredged channel and got over on the Essex shore. A useful breeze came in from north-east and we slowly beat along the line of buoys that mark the edge of the Maplin Sands. I was surprised to see a fast runabout anchored off the Blacktail Spit. They did not seem to want to see us and I wondered if they were smuggling. It is a good spot for a rendezvous but a queer place to moor for the night. Even with this light wind against the tide she was rolling like a cow. It became obvious that there was no chance of getting round the Whittaker Beacon before the flood set in and on my assurance that I knew of a safe anchorage, Tony turned in. At 0015 hrs I eased over into a shallow gut in the sands north-west of the Maplin Spit, known I believe, as

Abraham's Bosom and once popular with bargemen, to anchor for the night. Once the tide began to flood it was very quiet there and I slept like a log.

It was 0700 hrs when we looked out on Sunday morning to find ourselves isolated in a little world of our own.

'Where is the sea wall,' said Tony after peeping hard into the light haze clothing the smooth water all around us.

'About three miles over there!' I replied, pointing north-west.

A hint of a breeze from south-east lasted just long enough to tempt us into getting underway, but in any case it was nearly high water and soon the faithful, ever reliable tide would start to ebb north-east, the way we had to go. Tony had watched carefully as I got the anchor effortlessly and noted that it came up spotlessly clean. He confessed later that for the next three hours he suspected that we had been drifting all night with the anchor just hanging down in the water while he had slept imagining a sea wall close to hand. It was 1000 hrs before the Ridge buoy loomed out of the mist to give us a fix. The breeze eventually came in from the south-east and we ran through the Spitway at low water, had a walk on the Buxey Sand and so back to the River Blackwater expecting an easy sail home. You never can tell with the east coast sailing. Off Sales Point the wind went round one hundred and eighty degrees in fifteen minutes and we close reefed for a beat home in south-west 6/7 to reach the mooring at 1830 hrs just forty-eight hours out, having sailed ninety-six miles in a very calm weekend.

Chapter Eighteen

A Pattern of Islands, Thames Style

This was the month of June in all her glory, long hot days, light winds and short warm nights. The Dinghy Cruising Association had a weekend rally planned at Paglesham on the River Roach for Saturday the seventh but this was far too modest a task for the little gaff cutter *Shoal Waters* as she waited on the mud at Heybridge, twenty-five miles away, for the Friday evening tide that would free her to roam the wide Thames Estuary for fifty glorious hours. The forecast was for light winds from the north-west. The offshore breeze in this area blows from this direction and the afternoon breeze comes in from the south-east. Thus the probability was that we would get a lively north-westerly overnight, a long calm around midday as the forecast north-westerly argued matters out with the growing onshore breeze from the south-east, until it triumphed by teatime and blew until sunset.

A trip that had fascinated me for years was the idea of taking the ebb tide out of the Blackwater to the Spitway, the flood tide to the Medway and into the West Swale at HW, where the tide going east for the first of the ebb would sweep her through to Harty Ferry ready to take the next flood back to Essex. Little did I know that other minds were working on other interesting routes to the rally that would take them over the Maplin Sands and into Havengore Creek. Most important of all for dinghy cruising, there were plenty of alternatives if the going got tough, or the crew just got tired. She could slip down through the Rays'n Channel to the Crouch, go through the Spitway and down the Whittaker Channel, take the morning flood directly into Havengore Creek or even anchor in the Medway and sail straight back to Essex over the afternoon flood without rounding the Isle of Sheppey.

High water was 1900 hrs Friday and a light air from the north-west carried her smoothly down the river with the evening ebb. I snoozed while Joy steered. She was worried at our apparent slow progress but at 2100 hrs I pointed out that we had made good four knots to the power station at Bradwell. Strong stuff these tides! As night closed in we found ourselves in company with several large boats also set for a night passage. Just before midnight *Shoal Waters* passed slowly through the Spitway and pointed her bowsprit south. The 0015 hrs forecast gave light airs from the north-west.

Gradually the wind rose to the top of force three sending the little cutter racing along the edge of the sands with the young flood like a scalded cat. Joy looked out at 2000 hrs to see the great iron cardinal buoy at Maplin Spit sweep by and stayed until 0300 hrs by which time the Blacktail Spit was abeam and dawn well on the way. The great chimney on the Isle of Gain power station beckoned us onto the Medway and it looked like an easy leap, but the chart showed that we still had a good eight miles to go and now we were hard on the wind. I would have liked to see the Thames a little smoother at this fragile hour but progress was good and at 0510 hrs *Shoal Waters* swept through between the Medway forts and headed down the Swale, glad to be in smooth water again. The sleeping yachts on Queenborough's crowded moorings flashed by and at 0600 hrs the traditional bucket went up to the masthead for the bridge-keeper at Kingsferry.

The sun came out from behind a cloud bank on the eastern horizon and Joy appeared to brew up as I jilled about for half an hour, waiting for the massive bridge to rise up between the tall piers and let us carry on eastward with the last of the flood. Once safely through, Joy took the helm and I got an hour's sleep to wake as the moorings at Harty Ferry came abeam. The anchor went down a hundred yards north-west of the Sand End buoy, the eggs and bacon went into the frying pan and we cleared our bunks ready for some more kip.

At first the ebb tide roared by, but by 1030 hrs only a sluggish stream kept *Shoal Waters* pointing whence she had come and a great whale of a sandbank loomed to port for we were well out of the main channel which runs along the south shore. The sun scorched down and was already killing off the wind. With low water at 1400 hrs it should have been possible to leave as late as 1300 hrs if the wind held, but it was obviously not going to oblige. She joined the procession of yachts leaving the East Swale to find a few moments of very local southerly offshore wind and then a long slow glide out onto the broad Thames, juggling with the Ghoster (an old name now reinvented as a cruising shute) to woo each cat's-paw until the wind came in from the east at about 1600 hrs. Then the little lady got weaving and danced across the main shipping lanes and on over the covering Maplin Sands to reach the Broomway, the ancient road to Foulness Island, at 1800 hrs with an inch or two under her keel. It was too early for the bridge keeper to be on duty so we enjoyed a steak supper at anchor a few hundred yards to seaward of the rickety iron structure. Suddenly two sails appeared at the entrance to the creek from the north. I recognised *Wellington* the fourteen foot *Skipper* owned by David and Gail McClellan and a *Mirror dinghy* sailed by Stewart Duncan. They had launched at Fambridge early in the day and sailed round the Whittaker Beacon at low water, a trip to the rally of some thirty-two miles. Of course, if conditions had not been suitable they could have shortened the trip by turning down into the Roach from the Crouch and got to Paglesham direct. We threw them a line and there was just enough time for tea all round before the bridge keeper appeared. When the old iron road and rail bridge went up we had to beat through for the wind inland was still westerly. As the sun went down the flotilla beat slowly through the creeks west of Potton Island to arrive at Paglesham where they beached on the mud near the hard as the ebb gathered speed. *Gypsy* a twenty-three foot open boat owned and built by Eva Grotto on whaler lines (four sheets of ply long) had already arrived from Harwich.

Sunday dawned warm and sunny, *Gypsy* left well before HW as Eric Coleman, the founder of the Dinghy Cruising Association, arrived from Maldon in *Rebel* his own design for a cruising dinghy. Joy fried up sausages for hot dogs all round (bring your own bread) as we chatted away the rest of the flood tide. The five boats had covered some two hundred miles between them getting to this Rally.

Shoal Waters and *Rebel* had to leave on the top of the tide for the Blackwater. Now we never race in the DCA but it has to be admitted that whenever two or more craft sail in company from point 'A' the respective owners have a pretty clear idea of the order in which they should arrive at point 'B', particularly as so many of them have designed or adapted their own boats. Someone on shore shouted a sacrilegious 'Bang' as we left. In fact varying winds showed *Shoal Waters* alternatively the stern and bow of *Rebel* until a thunderstorm off Stone put her ahead for the last reach past Northey Island where we anchored to pack up and wait for the evening tide to cover our moorings. As the saying goes, the smaller the boat the better the sport. On idyllic weekends like that, I really believe it!

Chapter Nineteen

Three Days of Freedom

On the debit side it was three o'clock on an early May
morning and the air outside the cabin struck distinctly
chilly after the warmth of a sleeping bag – two sleeping
bags, in fact. On the credit side it was high tide and *Shoal
Waters* rode high above the saltings off the ballast hole at the
Blackwater SC at Heybridge. The moon was just past full
(hence the spring tide) and playing hide-and-seek in a sky
half full of clouds. A light wind drifted in from the south-
west, not enough to ruffle the water in the lee of the sea
wall, but sparkling ripples in the track of the moon
promised more wind out in the river. Most important of
all, I had Friday free to add to the weekend; three whole
days of freedom with the wide Thames Estuary at my
pleasure: just me and the best little cruiser on this coast.
Previous trips this year had taken her up the Crouch to
Battlesbridge and across the Thames to the Medway. Now
for the Harwich area.

Shoal Waters does not usually carry a topsail during the
dark hours but this night the sail would be needed with a
spring ebb carrying her away from what little breeze there
was. In the darkness the sheet somehow found its way
round the halyard, but it set well enough for downwind
work. The mooring buoy splashed overboard into the dark

satin water and we glided out on to the broad estuary. I settled back in my duffel coat and began to sort out the early morning stars. Overhead a very bright white heavenly body defied the moonlight. It could only be Jupiter. Another was confirmed as Vega when my binoculars picked out a double star a couple of degrees away, and in the gaps in the clouds could be seen the rest of Patrick Moore's summer triangle.

Dawn was well on the way as *Shoal Waters* swept past Bradwell power station. A sailing barge anchored over on the Mersea shore enriched the scene as I brewed up in what would be the last smooth sheltered water for some hours. The flash of the Bench Head buoy (still white, but not for many more weeks with the new system starting any day) glinted palely in the dawn and then suddenly it was daylight. The wind was rising and the little cutter was going like a train. For some years I had been carrying flash gear for my camera in case a chance came along to climb the Old Gunfleet Light Tower on the sand of the same name, a few miles south-east of Walton. This seemed as good a chance as any and we eased over towards the Spitway to pass down the Swin, for the sands dry on the Wallet side and the tower can only be approached from the east at low water. The sun rose to perfection, decorating the blue of the sea with a broad swathe of molten gold.

It is a long haul from the Swin Spitway buoy to the West Gunfleet starboard buoy. The sea-marks have been thinned out in this area since sailing craft ceased trading, for the motor craft prefer the narrower, deeper Barrow Deep. Thanks to the fair wind, the buoy was in sight by 0630 hrs and astern twenty minutes later, cheering me no end with firm evidence of a strong tidal stream going my way very fast. The forecast gave south-westerly four going westerly later.

The old gunfleet light tower guided shipping in this area for many years up to the Second World War, but it has a strangely modern look, almost like a moon landing craft, with its spidery, long legged silhouette. Within the triangle of the port shrouds and the mast it grew rapidly from a hazy, almost ethereal, tiny triangle just visible on the distant horizon, into a firm, bold and then massive iron structure that towered over the topsail. It was 0750 hrs when *Shoal Waters* arrived just before low water. I sailed round to assess the problem and found more swell than one would have wished (about two feet from trough to crest). The ladder is on the eastern side which makes boarding dangerous with the wind in the east. *Shoal Waters* anchored to windward and at the third attempt found the right spot so that the boat dropped back on the cable to lay about ten yards from the ladder. The kedge, an eight pound fisherman, hooked onto the structure on the second throw and thus the little boat could be pulled into the ladder which slopes inwards as the structure narrows. The metal has rusted away from the lowest horizontal member at about the level of low water springs. There seemed to be a danger that once my weight was put upon it, the ladder could bend in from the upper end and leave me five feet or more away from the frame, safety and my boat. I first put a strong line round the lower rung and the horizontal member and then armed with camera and flash gear, I stepped onto the ladder and kicked the boat away. She lay back on her anchor cable clear of the tower but could be pulled to the ladder when wanted by a lazy painter to a cleat on the stern.

The lower rungs, under water more often than out of it, are covered with barnacles and need careful handling, for the rims of the shells are sharp. Once above the high water mark, bird lime becomes the trouble and as the hand rails look very dodgy, 'tread carefully' is the watchword. The boat was riding quietly, well clear of the structure. Through the door in the bottom of the capsule, in which three men lived for weeks at a time, moon craft fashion, I found that the internal fittings had been vandalised since my last visit. The kitchen stove, which had once seemed to be the heart of the two story accommodation had gone and partitions were broken down. Two of the roomy bunks were intact. Out in the bright sunlight on top, I found the base of the light with bullet holes still there as evidence of wartime shoot-ups by enemy aircraft and the perimeter rails shakier then ever. Presumably some sort of engine must have driven the light or shades to give the flashing effect. The trolley wheels are still there but the light itself seems to have gone over the side judging by the gap in the rails. Fascinating as the place was, it was good to get back on little *Shoal Waters*, retrieve the lines, weigh and stow the anchor, and unfurl the headsails to blow due north towards the sands now covering rapidly with the rising tide. I dropped the hook in three feet of water and settled down to a steak breakfast in just about as perfect a situation as one could imagine, cheered by the thought of colleagues at the office just getting into their stride for the day.

By the time that breakfast had been eaten and cleared up, the boat was snubbing at her cable and the swell increasing fast as the water deepened. The banks between us and the Wallet were now covered with enough water for me to cross with the plate right up. This is known as the 'Tea Pot' system of reduction to soundings as distinct from the Admiralty graph system. By now the wind had got up to a good working breeze and the topsail was stowed before I got under way for Walton Backwaters under plain sail.

Two Ocean Youth Club ketches heading south with the young flood made a fine sight but other northbound modern cruisers with the wind astern and no spinnakers were making only slow headway past the Naze. *Shoal Waters* closed the coast and crept round the shoreline to pass through the gut between Walton Stone and the Pye Sand, saving a lot of time and, today, windward work. In Hamford water a squally patch seemed stationary overhead instead of sweeping over in the normal fashion and eventually we surrendered and pulled down a reef before beating steadily between Skippers Island and the wide marshes that stretch away towards Oakley, to Landmere and into the tidal canal to tie up to the fine stone wharf at Beaumont Quay. It is a far cry from most farmer's landing places, so often these days just a few rotting stakes, and the explanation is given on a stone plinth proclaiming that the quay was built in by the executors of Guys Hospital from some of the stones of Old London bridge when the 1176 structure was pulled down. The stones were brought back by sailing barges which had taken hay, straw and other fodder to London for the horses that thronged the streets of the capital. I suppose that in those days barges were the equivalent to the modern road tanker! The work involved in building the quay and digging the canal gives an idea of the importance of waterborne traffic in those far off days before the infernal combustion engine set the roads a-thunder.

I brewed up and then walked over to watch the tide running into the hold of the old barge *Rose* of Maldon rotting away on the saltings beyond the wharf. If only these old hulls could talk! There is a farmhouse and outbuildings some five hundred yards away but no signs of life today. It was almost as quiet and lonely a spot as the Gunfleet Light tower.

Just before the top of the tide *Shoal Waters* sailed back through the maze of saltings (this is no place to get neaped on the first of the ebb!) to pick up a mooring off the bird sanctuary at Skippers Island in time to listen to the 1400 hrs forecast give westerly three to four. With the whole of the broad estuary brim full (including part of the island itself where the sea wall is broken), a warm sun, a blue sky littered with white fluffy clouds and no other soul in sight, I could have sat in the cockpit with my glasses for hours but an afternoon zizz was the firm choice. There is a persistent rumour that I manage to go a long way in my small boat by never sleeping. Nothing could be further from the truth for I likes my kip, but once afloat am prepared to sleep or sail as the tides dictate in the manner of those who sailed these waters in the days of commercial sail.

There had been some talk of rain later but the sun was still shining at 1700 hrs. What a different world! The saltings loomed high on either hand, flanked with miniature cliffs and mud flats patrolled by seabirds. With one reef down *Shoal Waters* sailed on past Dovercourt and into Harwich, keeping close to the breakwater on the western edges of the entrance away from the shipping lanes. Now the sky was overcast with a light streak above the horizon. Harwich first stood out in sharp silhouette, its tall lookout towers having an almost 'Easter Island Statue' appearance. Close to the shore *Shoal Waters* dodged the tidal stream, twice being forced out by fingers of shingle, warned by an ever vigilant centre-plate which, in smooth water, acts unashamedly as an audible echo sounder cum instant draft reducer.

Harwich/Felixstowe/Parkstone Quay is a busy world these days, both in its own right and as the gateway to Ipswich. At the Guard buoy I did the school boy crossing act of looking right and then left before heading across the main channel to Shotley Spit. It is not far, but large craft travel fast here and can seem to appear from nowhere. Once in the lee of the Suffolk shore, the boat went over the ebb in fine style. A much larger yacht which had seemed to be catching up now began to drop astern rapidly as she had to keep out into the deeper water, and inevitably, the stronger foul tide. From Colimer Point *Shoal Waters* was on the wind, a long port tack and a short starboard and later, in the lee of the trees, the reef had to be shaken out. The sun showed itself a couple of times to cheer us on our way and just before the bottom of the tide the little cutter slid onto the mud, west of Pin Mill for the night.

Overnight, the rain came – and came – and came. It eased at dawn and at 0530 hrs *Shoal Waters* was under way again, either to take the flood up the coast or, if conditions were too rough, up the River Stour to Manningtree. Prospects looked bleak at first in Sea Reach, but after breakfast off Stoneheaps I sailed out to have a look at it in the best cruising traditions and found prospects improving. The sky cleared from the west and an idyllic trip up the Wallet in warm sunshine brought Colne Point abeam at 1310 hrs. A couple of coasters swung to their anchors off East Mersea, waiting for the tide right up to Colchester. *Shoal Waters* had a more modest objective, the tide mill at Thorrington at the head of Alresford Creek. The entrance, once spanned by a swing bridge in the days of the 'crab and winkle' railway line to Brightlingsea, is very tricky, winding among extensive mud flats but we found it well marked with withies, a sure sign that the boat population inside is rising fast. The lovely old barge jetty still stands there at the end of an aerial ropeway and the ford, once the main road from Brightlingsea to Colchester for horse drawn traffic, was a busy scene with some people fitting out, and others just afternoon water watching. A few minutes later *Shoal Waters* was alone again as the creek meandered, growing ever more winding and narrow, past woods and strangely enough, Brightlingsea church. Even this stretch was marked with withies and at the mill I found a large motor-sailor, presumably the beneficiary.

Thorrington is just one more charming spot that makes the chief problem when describing this cruising area the lack of sufficient superlatives to do justice to the scenery. The skeleton of the water wheel is still there, but the water in the pool is now fresh water and silting up fast. How they ever worked barges up there is a mystery, although presumably the creek has silted up since the mill was built, cutting off the tidal scour from the upper reaches, and of course many early barges were quite small for those that have survived are the biggest and best of the breed. *Shoal Waters* left with the tide and joined the main river for a beat over the ebb to Wivenhoe before running back into Alresford Creek to moor for the night near the old sand jetty. Once she had dried out I walked along the rope (or at least along the ground underneath it), to the pit to fathom exactly how it worked. Things like Concorde and calculators leave me cold for they are just beyond my comprehension, but things like this, sort of giant Meccano sets, delight me. In actual fact the runway is younger than I am, having been built in 1932 – but even that is getting old now.

More rain overnight, and so we left at 0600 hrs to get clear before the creek dried out. After breakfast off East

Mersea over the last of the ebb, the sky cleared as the wind obligingly veered north-west to let us point straight into the Blackwater river, the mooring, home and that office desk on the morrow.

Chapter Twenty

Voyage into Constable Country

During the 1969 Boat Show I learnt from the Inland Waterway Association stand that it was still possible to get through the derelict lock at Brantham onto the canalised River Stour as far as the lock gates at Flatford in the heart of Constable country. It promised an interesting and challenging trip to reach Flatford from Heybridge and return over one weekend. An exploratory trip in the middle of April, as far as the lock gates, showed a further problem: a bridge had been built over the lower gates about a foot above the lock walls. The upper gates were permanently open but the lower ones maintained the water in the river about a foot below High Water Ordinary Springs. I watched the tide rise level with the water in the river, whereupon the lower gates opened and salt water swept upstream raising the water level about a foot during the last hour of the flood. Once the ebb set in the gates snapped shut. There might be just enough room to get through with the mast right down as low as possible. To get as much headroom as possible it would have to be done the moment the gates could be opened. It would not do to get the boat stuck under as the tide rose! The easiest way would be to get someone local to tie the bottom gates open on the previous high water but this might raise problems upstream.

A determined effort a fortnight later to coincide with the Stour Preservation Society's AGM petered out in thick fog early on Saturday morning. Friday 16 May did not seem very promising. High water was at 0130 hrs on Saturday morning so I was unable to get right away on Friday evening and had to wait until the returning tide reached *Shoal Waters* at 2330 hrs. I waded out to the boat over the mud and got a little sleep. It was calm as the tide reached her but there seemed to a be a little breeze from the south-west (as forecast) and I decided to get away, although the flood tide would be against me for two and a half hours. The clink-clink-clink of the anchor windlass of a barge rang out across the silent river as I washed the mud from my water boots under a canopy of stars.

As I crept along the shore past Mill Beach the breeze grew steadily and by the time I cut across Osea Island causeway (sailing behind the island dodges the strong flood tide in the narrows on the southern side), the boat was going like a train. Half an hour later off Thirslet Spit I had to pull down a reef. The ebb set in as I reached Mersea Island and it was quite lively off the entrance to the River Colne. In smoother water along the St Osyth shore, the water was black as ink and the bow wave was phosphorescent. Behind me the wake came away from the rudder like a blaze of clear fire. This passage is always enlivened by the possibility of sailing the five miles between Clacton and Walton piers in less than one hour. This time I did it with three minutes to spare.

By this time dawn was evident, but clouds took over the sky after a red sunrise and things looked bleak indeed as I passed into Harwich at 0530 hrs to anchor for an hour's sleep just inside the breakwater. It was far too rough to cook breakfast there, so I close reefed the main, set the small jib and sailed round Harwich to beat up the Stour. The wind had gone westerly, bringing it on the nose, and already there were white horses on the waves as the young flood met the rising wind. I was glad to creep into the mud flats beyond Parkeston Quay and anchor for about half an hour to get some thin cut steaks into the frying pan with a dab of butter. Then on past Mistley and Manningtree to Cattawade which I reached at 1100 hrs. I ran her bows into mud on the western bank. By the time I had the mast down she was well afloat, and with the aid of the wind, which was now behind me on this reach, and an eight foot sounding pole, made fine progress under the rail bridge and the historic red brick Cattawade bridge. Then I got the sails up again for a half mile beat up the winding river to the lock.

Inspection showed that the level of the water in the river above the lock was the same as it had been a month ago and thus I should have the same headroom. I have since realised that a paddle of the lock gates leaks and two other gaps in the river bank allow fresh water to escape in other places. This, combined with a steady inflow over the weir at Flatford, means that the level of the water between the mill and Brantham is constant except for an hour before and after the highest tides. Down came the mast. Normally I lower it onto the boom in the scissors-type crutch which stands on the afterdeck for most bridges. For lower ones I can stand the crutch on the stern seat some nine inches lower, but now the mast had to come right down on the cabin hatch. Even this did not look low enough, so I removed the hatch completely and this gave another three inches. I manoeuvred *Shoal Waters* so that her bowsprit poked expectantly into the apex of the lock gates and climbed onto a cross member of the gates about three feet from the top. Standing thus I could reach the girders of the bridge and force the gates open those precious seconds early while the water above was marginally higher than the rising tide.

No luck at first, but as the water flooded over the toes of my water-boots, the right-hand gate opened and then the left. I leapt onto the boat and shoved her under. There was no time to loose for if she would not clear the bridge, she had to be got out of the lock in quick time before the flooding tide jammed her there. She went smoothly under as I ducked into the cockpit and was then able to pole her to the far side of the lock. Getting the mast up again proved a bit of a puzzle as lowering it right down had tangled the rigging up with fittings on the boat and I had to make three attempts before she cleared everything. It was a beat out of the lock so I decided to pole her out through the upper gates before putting up the sails. She swung over and jammed. It took all my might sitting on the lock wall and pushing with my legs to free her. Then away for the beat to Flatford.

The river is very shallow at the edges, and I had to use the centre-plate hoist regularly. It was just 1420 hrs as I moored up against the lock gates near the famous mill. A tourist about to take a shot of the mill lowered his camera until I sailed past! The afternoon passed pleasantly enough. I ought to have slept, for there was a busy night ahead, but after an hour or so I gave up and joined the steady stream of visitors around this delightful spot. At 1800 hrs the forecast spoke of the wind going north-west which suited me very well and I got under way for the trip back to the lock. The sun came out and it was a pleasant fair-wind trip, arriving at the lock at 1900 hrs. I anchored inside the upper gates (this lock is circular with grass banks), and crawled into my sleeping bag for there was little to be done until midnight.

At 0010 hrs I got dressed, made a cup of tea and walked over to the lock gates to find that the tide was well on its way. After lowering the gear, I poled the boat under the bridge and took a line over the gates to a bollard, leaving a long line ready to carry round the pool once she was through. The sky was dark and the wind blew strongly from the north. I have never needed a thunderstorm less and fortunately only got a little drizzle. Climbing out along the gates was far less attractive in the dark with the boat on the other side. If I slipped back into the water I would stand little chance in oilskins and water-boots. I had thought of my safety harness but it would get in the way and I had to be able to move fast. Slowly the water rose over my boots on the !edge. I tested the gate regularly, at first without success; then the right-hand gate moved, letting water surge downstream and bringing the bowsprit through between the gates. As I shifted my grip the gate nearly slummed shut on it. A final heave, and the gate went right back to the wall. I climbed onto the bridge and down onto the other gate. It moved easily and I pulled the boat through; jumped onto the stern, thence onto the lock wall, cast off the line from the bollard, and struggled through the reed beds round the pool to pull her clear of the current which would be racing up through the gates in a few minutes.

After a pause for breath and a sigh of relief, the mast went up smoothly and I settled back in the cockpit for a smooth sail to Cattawade. She was still close reefed but there was wind enough to take her over the flood tide. Down mast again, this time with plenty of light from the plastics factory at Brantham and once again a fair wind to take her under the road and rail bridges. As the ebb set in and the 0200 hrs forecast came over the radio I was sitting comfortably at the helm for the trip home. The forecast told of northerly winds, force five to seven and up to eight in places. Then out reefs for a steady trip down the dark silent river towards the loom of light above busy Felixstowe. I didn't trouble about navigation lights (paraffin), as it would be dawn by the time I reached Harwich. Once clear of the harbour, the wind rose again, but I was soon round the Naze in the lee of the shore, racing along in smooth water. The cold wind and light drizzle were a small price to pay for a fair wind home. A furious thunderstorm passed well ahead over Mersea as I crossed the Colne Bar and by 1100 hrs I was anchoring off Osea Island for a wash and a meal before picking up to my mooring at 1300 hrs.

Chapter Twenty-One
Don't Just Sit There; See Something!

Sailing is fun anyway. The sheer joy of a little ship wooing the winds to travel over the waves is reward enough in itself, but the small boat sailor on the restless waters of the Thames Estuary gets an almost unlimited bonus from the backcloth against which he sails. Not for him the endless lonely days of sea and sky of the ocean traveller. Hour by hour an enthralling panorama of fauna, flora, trade ancient and modern, relics of wars fought yesterday and a thousand years ago, maritime architecture from St Peter's on the Wall circa 675 AD, to the modern power station at the Isle of Grain and the most enduring of all, sea defences from ancient grass banks long since breached, to today's massive Woolwich Barrier, unfolds before him.

Above it all is the dome of the sky with little high ground to obscure the horizon. Clear skies, dull grey ones, skies with all manner of cloud patterns, skies set on fire by wild dawns and glorious sunsets, skies dominated by the full moon, skies on moonless nights when the stars burn all the brighter to make up for the absence of their lunar mistress, warm friendly skies that make you want to sail for ever, grim threatening skies that send you scurrying into the nearest harbour and, yes let's be honest, dreary characterless skies that impose their mood on you and your little ship.

Moonlight sailing needs no advertisement, but sailing at night is so much more rewarding to the sailor who can pick out the major stars and constellations. The season starts with Leo, the lion dominating the cold night air. By mid-summer the evening sky brings out bright white Vega and the summer triangle it forms with Deneb and Altair. The names of the stars, as distinct from the names of the patterns they form, are of Arab origin. While admiring them from a small boat in the Thames Estuary, it is interesting to think back to the men who studied and named them as they rode their ships of the desert in ages past. As the days begin to shorten the Severn Sisters climb into the morning sky above the mist, followed by the red star Aldebaran, the eye of the bull in Taurus, and later in the month the greatest constellation of them all, Orion the hunter. Soon the line of stars that make up his belt will lead down left to Sirius, the dog star which tells us that we are in the dog days of August. An extra incentive at the beginning of that month is the abundance of shooting stars which may only be bits of dust but very beautiful dust as they hurtle across the sparkling sky. By autumn the great square of Andromeda with its giant nebula completes a programme of 'onboard entertainment' to rival anything provided for the passengers on jumbo jets by the film industry. While all this is happening the Great Bear circles the Pole star in the northern sky and the moon, Venus, Jupiter and Mars take turns on stage in the southern sky. I could never interpret the circular maps of the sky, for it must be admitted that none of the constellations look anything like the mythological characters after whom they are named. Then I bought Patrick Moore's *Naked Eye Astronomy* in which he shows the sky in two half spheres, north and south, for every two hours of each month throughout the year. Before reading it I had never realised that the northern stars are always there, merely changing position relative to the Pole star, while the southern stars hide away in turn throughout the year to give regular seasonal patterns. It is well worth the effort to sort out the basic shapes. So many town dwellers hardly ever look up into the night sky and even if they do, the magic is quite hidden by the orange glare of street lights. I am sure that if the clouds only parted once every ten or twenty years to reveal the star spangled heavens, it would be an event which few people on earth would miss. During the passage of the Bale-Bopp comet, the clear, crisp view I enjoyed among the open marshes of the estuary contrasted vividly with the dull, watery sightings at home on shore where light pollution turns the night sky into a dull orange soup.

The maritime lowlands of Suffolk, Essex and Kent live in a constant state of siege from the restless sea. They depend for their protection on a fragile lip of sea wall that winds its patient way round the outer fringes of the marshes, tracing the intricate pattern of creeks and rivers with a firm solid line. The sea walls along the comparatively narrow Suffolk rivers are still much as they have been since they were first built several hundred years ago, just a ridge of earth covered with rough grass. In Essex the walls were faced with Kentish ragstone brought across the Thames from the upper Medway. It was still possible, in the late seventies, to see the shoots through which the vessels were loaded just below Allington lock. It must have been a cruel trade for the barges, with those sharp stones hurtling down into the hold.

The wider the area of open water the walls looked out on, the more elaborate the facing. Nowadays small square concrete slabs are used held together only by a mixture of tar, sand and asbestos ladled boiling hot into the joints. This allows the whole surface to move as the clay of which the sea walls are built shrinks in the heat of summer and expands again with the winter rains. Small gangs of hardy, weather beaten men are always at work somewhere along the coast during the week. The weekend yachtsman can spot their progress by the fresh white gleam of the new slabs and the silhouettes of the coppers, in which the tar mixture is boiled, standing out above the top of the sea wall against the setting sun. The lower blocks are much heavier than the upper ones. Fixing them in place is a skilled job, as was demonstrated by a local householder with a garden adjoining the river who faced the crumbling soil at the water's edge with these blocks himself. Within a year or two they were collapsing into the mud. The inside of the marina at Bradwell was lined with these slabs and they started slipping into the water almost as soon as the first boats arrived at the pontoons. A recent development has been the use of lighters, now redundant on the London river, to protect the more exposed stretches of sea wall from attack by the North Sea. They are loaded with mud and sunk on the flats about a quarter of a mile out from the sea wall. Then they are topped up with mud and a layer of shingle to make nesting sites for terns. The latter idea was foolish indeed, for it was obvious to anyone with the slightest knowledge of the way of the waves that the first easterly gales would half empty them. It happened the first winter. Nevertheless, sixteen of them out on the Denghie flats make a delightful drying harbour for a small boat 'who wants to be alone'.

Extensive brickworks thrived for many years along the Essex and Medway coasts, sending millions of bricks into expanding London and to tiny coastal villages growing rapidly into thriving seaside resorts with the advent of new piers where the paddle steamers unloaded holiday makers and day trippers. The 'South End' of the isolated marshland hamlet of Prittlewell grew so fast and so big that few people today have heard of the original village. Bent and distorted bricks not fit for sale found a home in the nearby sea walls and stretches can still be found in the quieter reaches of some creeks. A study of the sea walls from a small boat gives a sobering warning that man's grip on this coast is far from total. Many hundreds of acres have already gone back to the sea, Bridgemarsh Island in the Crouch, half of Northey Island in the Blackwater, Pewit Island and half of Skippers Island in Walton Backwaters and wide tracts of land at the head of the rivers Deben and Alde. Some of the last named areas have been lost within the reign of *Shoal Waters* from whose cockpit I once watched people strolling along sea walls where today there are gullies six feet deep, and the triumphant tide surges in and out like a mill race. Stakes hardened by fire were used in the original sea walls to buttress the clay against the shock of the battering waves and where the soil has been washed away, they remain today, hard as iron, a menace to any small boats that run onto them. At last the powers that be have admitted defeat and realised that they cannot win. Two areas have already been reopened to the sea on the River Blackwater where the sea walls, already in need of expensive repairs, only protect small parcels of land.

Sea walls are lonely places. They provide footpaths for walkers, family parties taking a Sunday stroll near built-up areas and sturdy hikers leaning the into wind as they complete the long winding trip from one access point to the next. The fifteen mile walk from Burnham to Bradwell is a particular challenge but at least it is flat. At times cattle and sheep, or better still horses, grazing the protected pastures will spare a moment to walk along the top of the sea wall and admire a passing boat. Perhaps sea walls look their best when hiding the hull of a spritsail barge so that the brown sails seem to grow out of the coarse grass. In some places the walls drop sheer into salt water and develop a skirt of bubbly-leaved seaweed, but more often the outer face stands on the mud flats or a shelf of rough grass known as saltings. These only cover at full and new moon when spring tides surge into the estuary and provide a precarious foothold for a crude but not unattractive flora, the best of which are the sea pinks in June and sea lavender in late July and early August. Individual blooms are never likely to grace the Chelsea flower show but when they grow in profusion they are a breathtakingly lovely sight.

The whole area teems with sea birds, some resident, some winter or summer visitors and others merely calling in on their annual travels. Not for the small boat sailor the cold draughty hides along the shores of the bird sanctuaries. From his little craft, whether at anchor or aground, he can watch the bird life in warm comfort, with endless hot food and drinks to hand when the mood takes him. The solitary heron is the most ubiquitous of all and found everywhere, from bleak saltmarshes to the deserted canals sneaking through London and the busy Norfolk Broads. At the other extreme are the Brent geese who dominate the area in the winter through sheer numbers. *Shoal Waters* likes to get afloat in the spring in time to wish them well on their journey north and accepts that it is time to lay up once they return.

Of course there are some parts of the coast where the land is above sea level and no wall is needed, but the low cliffs are of soft materials rather than stone or granite and constantly erode unless protected. Built-up areas are safe but at the Naze and on the northern face of the Isle of Sheppey unprotected land constantly slips into the sea. Recent proposals to protect more of the Naze met with vigorous opposition from keen geologists and fossil hunters who regard this as a prime site. No account of the coastline would be complete without a mention of shingle banks. In Essex the few shingle outcrops where one can get ashore at all states of the tide without having to wade through mud are known as 'Stones'. Hence Steeple Stone, East Mersea Stone, Stone Point etc. Much of the Suffolk coast is shingle, miles and miles of it with hardly any distinguishing features on the shore. One small cluster of cottages on the waters edge is actually called Shingle Street. The round stones move constantly south and provide the perfect materials for the swift ebb tides of the rivers Deben and Ore pouring out in a south-easterly direction, where they meet the ebb running north-east up the coast, to fashion a fresh puzzle of banks and channels for yachtsmen to unravel when they enter those rivers for the first time each spring. Both rivers had pilots for commercial craft up to the First World War and earlier yachtsmen seemed to have used them. Today they are well buoyed and leading marks have been installed.

Two thousand years of warfare has left its scars on the Thames Estuary. When the Romans first landed under Julius Caesar in Pegwell Bay south of modern Ramsgate, the Isle of Thanet was indeed an island, and a broad estuary gave a comfortable route into the Thames that saved the hazardous passage round the chalk cliffs of the North

Foreland. To protect it they built a mighty castle at Richborough from which Roman Britain was ruled for many years. Today its ruined walls still watch over the River Stour and the route to Forditch, the port of Canterbury. Other forts were built at Bradwell and Burgh Castle near Yarmouth to protect the shore from some fellows called Saxons. All that remains of Orthona, the fort at Bradwell, which was built just above sea level, is the early church, St Cedd, built in the western gateway, probably with material from the fort.

After the Saxons came the Vikings and then the Danes, but little of their building was substantial enough to last. A few burial mounds and some Nordic names along the coast, such as the Nass Spit at Mersea is all we have, plus an unmeasurable amount of salt blood in our veins. William the Conqueror built the Tower of London and in the feudal age that followed many others were built, among them Hadleigh, Orford, Rochester and Upnor. When gunpowder made them largely obsolete, some of that gunpowder was made on the marshes at Ore Creek near Faversham, under license from Henry VIII. Tilbury fort, of Queen Elizabeth fame, still manages to peep over the recently raised sea wall between the docks and power stations in Gravesend Reach. A small fort at East Mersea helped the Roundheads prevent Royalist ships raising the siege of Colchester during the Civil War, and there is still a pillbox there today left over from the Second World War.

The Dutch wars saw our sea power at its lowest ebb when the Dutch destroyed the partly built fort at Sheerness and sailed up the Medway as far as Upnor to cut out the Royal George and burn other vessels. It is still possible to follow the course of the battle in the museum at Upnor

Castle and stand on the platform from which they fired at the Dutch ships.

The threat of invasion by Napoleon Bonaparte brought a chain of brick Martello towers along the parts of the coast suitable for seaborne landings and most of them still stand. To get the hundreds of thousands of bricks to isolated stretches of coast with which to build the towers, flat bottomed lighters from the Thames were pressed into service and from them developed the Thames barges we know today. Later stone forts were built at Sheerness, Darnetness, Hooness, East Tilbury and Shornmead to protect the naval base at Chatham and London itself. The ill-fated cruisers *Hogue, Aboukir* and *Plessey* coaled in the Medway before sailing out into the North Sea in 1914 to give the Admiralty their first lesson in submarine warfare. In both world wars barges loaded with ammunition lay in these creeks ready to replenish warships, if the naval dockyards were damaged. On the Kentish River Stour, three quarters of a mile of piled jetty decays in the salt wind. In May 1916, twenty thousand men descended on the marshes here to build a port to take men and munitions to France. By November the first dumb barges left, and when hostilities ended three train ferries and other craft had moved a million tons of goods to war including 685 tanks. Over a dozen slipways were busy building barges and seaplane carriers. The Royal Flying Corps had a salvage area to rebuild war-damaged planes brought back from France.

Another threat of invasion in 1940 gave us a rash of pill boxes built into the sea walls and on low cliffs throughout the whole estuary. Some of them are now in the sea making a useful gauge of erosion locally. Even a few traces of the scaffolding built along the beaches in 1940 to deter landing craft can still be found. At Halvergate Island the first tests

on radar were carried out and the towers of the wartime
radar station at Bawdsey on the northern side of the
entrance to the Deben have provided a guide for yachtsmen
for over fifty years. German bombers found that they could
dodge the radar screen by coming in low over the water.
One morning they found great towers set out on the sands
with guns glazing. Today these towers still dominate the
estuary and mark sands with such delightful names as the
Red Sand, the Shivering Sands, the Knock John Sand and
the Tongue Sand. It never ceases to amuse me that 'My
Lords Commissioners of the Admiralty' take the view that
no one but an utter cad would ever navigate by these blocks
of flats all over the place and mark them with a tiny circle
on their charts. The buoys marking the position of the
towers are shown boldly and are the easiest ones in the area
to find. Just look for the towers and the buoys are right
alongside! In fairness it must be admitted that the buoys are
lit at night. Today sea gulls perch on the barrels of guns that
haven't seen a Heinkel or a Dornier for fifty years. Some of
those planes stayed in the estuary and can still be found
among the sands. I have often walked over to the wreck on
the Buxey Sand and understand that among the visitors has
been the German pilot. This was a war of midget
submarines and a great defence boom was built across the
mud flats on either side of the estuary to keep them out.
With D Day looming, every creek was crammed with
landing craft and two sailing clubs now use the fine
concrete hards built to service them. One section of the
Mulberry harbour broke up off Southend, east of the pier
and is still there today, but Kent takes pride of place for
wartime relics with the ten thousand ton *Richard
Montgomery* still loaded with explosives for D Day stranded
on the sands outside Sheerness. There is a constant fear of

its blowing up and they dare not try to move it. The locals are very sensitive about explosions for a battleship blew up in the dockyard in 1914. Today a chain supported by a ring of buoys keeps small craft away and local magistrates have warned that any small boat owner who sets off that lot be heavily fined; if they can find him!

The old gunfleet light tower, a pile lighthouse that flashed red over the sand of the same name up to the Second World War was shot up from the air never to light again. It is worth a climb to see the bullet holes. Harwich was a seaplane base from the start of aerial warfare and the hammer head crane that lifted them ashore was a sea-mark for forty years, until it was replaced by the high cranes of the modern Felixstowe container port. When I first sailed the area, the Medway and the Stour inside Harwich were crammed with silent tiers of rusting warships, and Sunderland flying boats still took off from Felixstowe.

I told in chapter fourteen how I met the cruiser Belfast on her way up to London. On a dreary Saturday morning in May 1954 *Zephyr* was one of just two yachts in the outer Thames to greet the brand new Royal Yacht *Britannia*, escorted by cruisers ahead and astern, as she carried HM the Queen to London on the last leg of a visit to Australia. Earlier still I seem to remember playing on the beach at Southend while HMS *Hood* and another capital warship laid out in the roads. Today one might be lucky enough to see a naval craft on a courtesy visit to London or some other centre. Noisy aircraft still crack and jump their way across the Suffolk skies but otherwise peace reigns supreme over these delightful waters and civilian vessels go about their business undisturbed.

Roman ships came to these Essex creeks to export corn to Germany. Water remained the cheapest form of transport right up to the First World War for places beyond the railhead. Many of the lines that reached the coast never made a profit and closed down long before Dr Beeching did his stuff. Every waterside village and hamlet has its quay, hythe, strand or staithe. (How many people in London realise that the Strand got its name because boats once moored there?) Their very heartbeat was the twice daily visit of the flood tide. Everything from coal to beer came by water. Hay and straw for London's horses went out from all sorts of wharves and jetties in isolated creeks and most marshland farms still have a green lane leading to a farmers landing place at the waterside. One farm at Mundon, White House farm, even had its own canal. The entrance is blocked off now but the cut remains. Water, both fresh and salt, was the power for mills long before wind and tide mills were found at the head of many creeks. Today we have just two left, Woodbridge and lonely Thorington Creek but many of the mill pools remain. I have already mentioned that brickworks and other trades such as cement works and foundries thrived together with boatyards galore. Places such as Slaughden on the Alde and Manningtree on the Stour sent fishing vessels as far as Iceland for cod. Several canals carried goods even further inland. Some are defunct but those to Tonbridge, Hertford, Bishops Stortford and Chelmsford provide an interesting experience for yachts small enough to negotiate them.

What a fascinating parade of sailing craft have traded on these waters since the Roman corn galleys, and they were not the first. Fortunately the last and most delightful of them all, the spritsail barges are still with us. They do not trade now, but everywhere you look someone is restoring something and Cook's Yard[5] at Maldon is probably as busy today as it ever was in the heyday of sail. Vast timbers are still steamed in an old-fashioned steam chest (is there such a thing as a newfangled one?), before being bent into place. A public footpath runs between the shed and the river so that the public who seem to prefer barges to spacecraft, have become something of a nuisance. When I looked in one summer's day, they had a large notice up.

'This wood is iroko.

Yes. It is expensive.

We give it three hours at number eight.' and several other standard answers to standard questions. Some of the best barge hulls became motor barges after the Second World War but are now being re-rigged as pleasure craft. Barges no longer bring corn to waterside mills from the Port of London or take stacks of hay back there loaded ten feet above the deck for London's horses. No barge makes the long run down to the 'Northern Indies' for cargoes of black diamonds' for the local gas works. Today's barges take out charter parties by the week or just for the weekend and assemble regularly for barge races around the coast throughout the season. The wharves and jetties they once traded to and from rot away in peace. Over the years *Shoal Waters* has taken me to most of them under sail and sail alone. It's been a delightful trip.

---

[5]Cash flow problems seem to have quietened things down as we go to print.

Chapter Twenty-Two

The Very End of the Season

The year 1975 had been such a wonderful one that I was reluctant to let it slip from my grasp. The sailing season was long over as I carried my gear out over the knee deep mud to *Shoal Waters* – in fact it was just twelve days before Christmas. There was a gale warning out of the Thames for westerly gales but the sun shone from a cloudless sky and in spite of the cold, I liked the look of things. The moon was nearly full and would be there to help *Shoal Waters* on her way if the few hours of daylight proved insufficient for her travels. High water was at 2000 hrs and there was time for a brew up and a chance to laze in the warmth of the radiant heater in the tiny cabin, before the tide began to roll in over the mudflats off the Blackwater SC just below the canal basin at Heybridge. As the first water lapped the boat at half flood the cockpit tent was folded away and a reef tied into the mainsail, ready to go. I cast off the mooring, unrolled the jib and waited for her to move. Suddenly, she slid out towards deeper water; down went the rudder and plate; I settled on the stern seat and snuggled into my duffel coat as we set off on a fine sail behind Osea Island over the last three hours of the flood. A night run to the Crouch seemed on the cards but the bitter cold soon highlighted the attractions of a mooring in West Mersea just above the wooden jetty off the hamlet known as Old Mersea City. The wind eased and the reef came out to help her work her way over the ebb tide in the Thornfleet Channel between Cobmarsh and Packing Shed islands to the inner harbour.

Both of the headsails are on Wykeham-Martin furling gear so they were no trouble to stow on arrival. The mainsail rattled down and was soon stowed and well lashed down into the boom crutch, for if the nor-west gale came as forecast, it would be pretty lively here at high water on the last of the flood. Then up cockpit tent and I was able to shed some of my layers of wool and crawl into the cabin. Tea first, and then a steak was sizzling on the single burner stove. By the time the steak was ready I had dug the hot water bottle out of my sleeping bag (filled before leaving the mooring) and poured it back into the kettle to heat up again. The plastic-covered bunk cushion gets chilly so I stood it up for a while with the radiant heater in front of it to warm it before unrolling my sleeping gear. The two sleeping bags are covered with the heavy duffel coat; into my pyjamas, a cup of Horlicks and so to sleep. I hardly noticed the boat move all night. Next morning the sun was rising clear above the pretty village clustered round its prominent church tower. The lightest of breezes came out of the north, ruffling the blue blue water. What gale?

Having no dinghy, I can only get ashore on a rising tide by going alongside a jetty. An hour before high water *Shoal Waters*, under headsails only, glided over to the long wooden jetty where members of a fishing party waiting for their craft lent a helpful hand with the mooring lines. The jetty was thick with frost and the whole place was like a fairyland in the bright sunshine. An hour later she was slipping seawards, aiming to go through the Spitway but 'gently gently' was to be the rule this trip. The wind died to the lightest of airs as we sailed through the Besum Fleet, past the old church standing guard over the wide entrance to the River Blackwater and out towards the battered, laid-up tanker *Aro*. It was a dead run to the Spitway and with the ebb carrying her away from what little wind there was, progress through the water was minimal, even with the topsail set, so *Shoal Waters* altered course due south down the inshore Ray Sand Channel which brought her onto a broad reach and filled the headsails. After midday the wind came in light but steady from west by north, the sun shone steadily from a blue sky, and the familiar land and sea-marks gradually came into view: St Peter's on the Wall at Sales Point, the wrecks on the flats, the Buxey Beacon over to seaward and eventually just before sunset, the Sunken Buxey buoy over the tail of the drying Buxey Sand and the Yellow Ray buoy. It was just 1800 hrs as I hooked onto a mooring below just Burnham in brilliant moonlight.

Thick fog shrouded the tea kettle's early whistle at about 0700 hrs, giving me time to settle back in the warm for a another snooze. It cleared just before the sun came up over the sea wall of Wallasea Island. The cockpit tent, stiff as a board, was covered with frost – as indeed was all the deck, mast and rigging – and only with difficulty and bitterly cold fingers could it be fought into a parcel to stow under the stern seat. Then a gentle beat to Burnham town jetty, largely on the tide wind, for a shopping expedition before getting under way to drift rather than sail slowly upstream with the last of the flood to work up an appetite for a steak breakfast with new bread rolls. Strangely, there was thick fog across the river below Wallasea Marina so *Shoal Waters* hung to a buoy in the sunshine and I feasted while waiting for the tide to turn. The radio told a sad tale of fog, frost, dangerous road conditions and chaotic air transport on shore. At 1000 hrs we dropped down past Burnham with the tide in almost flat calm A little wind came in off the mouth of the river three hours later and by low water a light breeze from due north grew steadily but firmly to take us through the shallow water of the Rays'n and on over the flood to round the Buxey Beacon at 1630 hrs, disturbing the cormorants on sentry duty. As darkness closed in there seemed little hope of reaching Brightlingsea that night so we settled for Mersea. *Shoal Waters* could point north north-west but with the flood tide this was obviously not going to be enough to clear the shallows on the Bradwell shore. An hour or so later the north-easternmost wreck on the flats loomed out ahead in the moonlight and I came onto port tack for fifteen minutes. The wind had risen to force 2 by this time and *Shoal Waters* rippled along under the moon in thrilling style. The red flash of the Nass beacon came up well to port and we closed the shore near the church, squared away into the Besum Fleet and picked up the first mooring buoy we came to. Mooring up was a little more difficult tonight as the tent was still frozen stiff but the cabin was as snug as ever.

Next morning I was woken by the hooter of a local fishing boat as she roared out into the promise of another perfect dawn. I struggled to the hatch to give him a cheery wave; they may let sleeping dogs lie but no fisherman lets a yachtsman sleep on. There was a fine breeze from the north or just west of north about force 2 and under full sail *Shoal Waters* made a chilly but idyllic trip to Brightlingsea at the top of the tide, where a walk ashore to fill up the water cans was complicated by the frozen tap at the top of the jetty.

The growing ebb was the signal to start back for home as the wind grew from the west and the first clouds of the holiday took over the sky. A grim red sun peeped under the cloud banks to light up the rusty sides of the *Aro* as *Shoal Waters* beat slowly past. It was 2000 hrs as, with the wind dying, she glided inshore of Osea Pier to anchor for the night.

Next day, in dull overcast weather, *Shoal Waters* sailed to Maldon for a last look at the Fullbridge. Timber no longer arrives at Sadds Yard by sea but motor barges still bring cargoes of wheat to the Green's Flour Mill and the thriving Maldon Crystal Salt company still sucks in river water to extract the salt. Sailing barges with bare masts and sprits lowered against the winter gales line the quay. I see that several are keeping up the old custom of hoisting Christmas trees to the masthead. Upstream all manner of yachts hide under their winter covers, some on the edge of the saltings, some along the old wharves and jetties and the lucky ones lifted high and dry on the banks. After a look into the dykes of flooded Northey Island, sending clouds of ducks and geese into the now sunny sky, *Shoal Waters* picked up her mooring at 1230 hrs. By 1430 the tide had left her and I walked ashore at the end a classic season.

Appendix One

Sailing 1996

			Miles
February	27	Bought trailer – transferred boat to trailer	
March	1	Launched	
	2/3	Completed gear – to Maldon	
	3/5	W Mersea – Dredger – E Mersea – St Peters pm – home	30
	15	Day trip to rivermouth	20
	17/20	Roach – Battlesbridge – Havengore – Colne Point	140
	23/25	Trailer to Broads – Thurne Mouth – Pleasure Boat Inn	15
	29/31	Yarmouth – Ranworth – S Walsham – Obey Mill	42
April	3/9	Salhouse – Barton – Hickling – Horsey – Hickling	50
	17/21	Martham – Horsey – Hickling – Potter – Hickling – Wayford Bridge – Wroxham – Upton – Acle	80
	25/27	Waxham Bridge – Acle	30

			Miles
May	29/2	Thorpe – night trip in fog over Breydon	80
	7/8	Working party – Obey Mill – Ant Mouth	10
	11/14	S Walsham – Obey Mill – Hickling – Horsey – Martham Corner	32
	19/21	Hickling – Horsey – Martham – Horning	35
	24/26	S Walsham – Upton – Hickling – Horsey – home	26
June	31/10	Horning – Acle – Eayford – Stalham – Burgh Castle – sailing on Breydon – Fenside	102
	14/18	Ranworth – Black Horse Bridge – Hickling – Horsey-Fenside – trail home	35

Total Broads miles = 537 = 470 = 610 nautical miles.

	19	Maldon	
	21	West Mersea – Colchester – Walton – Oakley Dock – Skippers Island – Manningtree – Home	105
	27/29	West Mersea	20
July	5	Maldon	
	8	Colne Point	24

			Miles
	9	BOAT ON TRAILER	24
	11/21	Hamble – Sailing at rally – Burlsdon –	56
		Newtown – Newport – Beauleu River – Hamble – Hythe – Home	
August	24/11	Hythe – Keyhaven – Folly – Newport	110
		Ryde – Newport – Folly – Newtown – Cowes Week – Newport – Cowes Town Jetty – Buckler's Hard – Ashlett – Hyde – Ashlett.	
		ON TO TRAILER and home	
	12	Round Northey and Maldon	10
	14	Round Osea and Fullbridge	10
	15	Ray Island – Tollesbury flood – Lion Creek – Strood – Bradwell flood	82
September	21/1	Ipswich – Manningtree – Harwich – Mistley – Walton – Deben – Alde – Butley River – Pyfleet – Club	200
	6/8	Round East Barrow – East Swale – Milton – Havengore	95
	13/16	Thirslet Beach – Stow Maris – Bridgemarsh – Havengore – Pyfleet – Club	100
	23/25	Wallet – Pyfleet – Fingrinhoe – Club	50

			Miles
	28	Maldon Rally	
October	30/2	St Peters – Club	40
	5/6	Tollesbury – Buxey Bn	27
	11/13	Sales Point – Bradwell – etc.	30
	26/27	Bradwell flood – club	15
November	11	Osea pier and Maldon in hazy calm	5
Total 108 nights on board			1609

Appendix Two

Cost of Sailing 1996

Subscriptions

Blackwater SC	75.00	(OAP Half Rate)
BSC Boat charges '95	118.00	
Old Gaffers Association	7.00	
Inland Waterways Association	12.00	
Wey & Arun Soc.	7.50	
Insurance	66.50	
Walton buoys	5.00	

Maintenance

Turps sub and sand paper	2.50
Varnish and masking tape	10.10
Sander sheets	1.25
Varnish	8.00
Wire brush	1.55
Turps sub	1.29
Mooring shackles	2.30
S/S bolts	5.85

Line	2.00
Deck paint	8.49
Marlin	5.79
Tallow	2.00
Chamy cloth	2.00
Shackle	0.25
Whipping	3.00
Shock cord	3.00
Tow rope for trailer	31.80
2 s/s Shackles	7.26

Fees etc.

Broads toll	21.75
Horsey Mere	2.00
Newport fees, 3 x £5	15.00
Beauleu River	4.00
Ryde	4.00
Cowes town wharf	4.00
Mistly Rally	7.00
Maldon Rally	7.00

Clothing

Blue shirts, 2	28.50
Guernsey sweater	50.00
Fuel	
Gaz – 5 x 6 lb	40.00

Miscellaneous

Solent chart	11.50
Solent tides	9.95
Portsmouth tide tables	0.50

Total for year =	£601.43	
108 nights afloat =	£5.57	per day
1609 miles =	37	pence per mile